Simple Story Selling

**How To Eliminate Writer's Block, and Write Stories That
Sell**

by
Rob Drummond

Simple Story Selling: How To Eliminate Writer's Block, and Write Stories That Sell

Second Edition

Copyright 2017 © The Confusion Clinic Limited.
By Rob Drummond

ISBN-13: 978-1548085292
ISBN-10: 1548085294

First published in Great Britain by The Confusion Clinic Limited.

You can contact us at:

info@truestoryselling.com
www.truestoryselling.com

Table of Contents

Acknowledgements

The kernel of the seven-step production process described in Part 2 comes from Sean D'Souza at Psychotactics. Specifically, the use of Evernote, the timeline stage, the 'one idea' and the reconnect are all ideas I took from Sean. Sean's website is www.psychotactics.com.

Serious students should consider reading Christopher Booker's *The Seven Basic Plots*. It's well worth at least a scan through to get the big ideas. *The Seven Basic Plots* is a big, dense book, but it completely changed the way I thought about literature.

The Hero with a Thousand Faces by Joseph Campbell has also influenced my thinking about storytelling, although I recommend reading this after *The Seven Basic Plots*.

The 'open sandwich' structure described in Part 2 was inspired by *Great Leads: The Six Easiest Ways to Start Any Sales Message* by John Forde and Michael Masterson.

Thanks to Ben and Jaya at the Mountain Training School (https://mountainguideschool.com) for letting me use their email as my tragedy example in Part 3.

See These Ideas At Work...

The ideas in this book are based on practical everyday experience, rather than lofty academic ideals. I practice what I teach, and write a daily email newsletter.

If you're not already subscribed, you can join for free at www.truestoryselling.com/daily.

When you sign up, you'll also get a free login to my collection of guides and webinar recordings, including:

- My *Email Marketing Tool Review*
- My *7-day Storytelling Crash Course*
- My *Story Selling Manifesto* webinar
- My *Six Rules of Story Selling* sequence

Why not do it now, before it slips your mind? The link again is www.truestoryselling.com/daily.

Introduction

This book is for people who sell high value products and services, where building trust over a potentially long period of time is an essential part of the sales process.

If you're a copywriter, this should describe the clients you work for. (Or the clients you want to work with).

In recent years I have noticed more people talking about storytelling in the marketing and copywriting world. Telling your story and 'being yourself' has suddenly become marketing best practice.

We intuitively know this advice contains some merit. We can feel the power of stories every time we read a book, or go to the movies. But how do we translate stories into business use? How do we tell stories in an engaging way, without becoming boring or irrelevant?

The answer to that question lies within these pages.

Over the last few years I have built up an insight from the world of literature as to what a good story ought to contain. You may not believe me right now, but all great stories do follow the same universal pattern.

This book is about applying this pattern to your own stories, so they become 'evergreen', and never go out of date. It is about writing compelling stories that communicate your value to interested prospects for years into the future.

Whether you are using email, direct mail or some other format, every communication should strengthen the relationship you have with your reader. The objectives are to:

1. Entertain the reader

2. Educate the reader
3. Upgrade your reader's level of thinking about your subject

Once you have achieved these three objectives, you will be in a strong position to present an offer, or a 'call to action'. Many marketing campaigns fail simply because insufficient trust has been established with the reader.

The three objectives are in order. You cannot educate a reader without first entertaining them, because you will lose their attention. And you cannot upgrade a reader's level of thinking without first educating them. Most companies underestimate how long this process can take.

As I'll explain, the most obvious role of stories is to entertain, but great stories also satisfy the other two objectives.

I have primarily focused on emails in this book as the format your stories will eventually take. The principles of storytelling do not change across different media. If you are preparing a speech, a presentation or a letter, the ideas in this book will apply equally well.

A note on masculine / feminine wording. At certain points in the book I talk about the 'hero' of the story, and actions 'he' has taken. I've done this because writing 'hero or heroine', 'he or she' would become cumbersome. I've used 'hero' and 'he' in this book to refer to characters of both sexes.

If it bothers you, feel free to mentally add 'hero or heroine' and 'he or she' as you read.

The book is best read chronologically, but if you are looking for a 'quick win', start with Part 2. Part 2 covers the seven-step production process for creating story-based marketing communications.

Let's start by first looking at why stories are so important.

Part 1: Why Tell Your Story?

As far as we know, humans are more developed than any other animal in our ability to imagine events and happenings through our mind's eye. Aristotle called this our ability to 'imitate' - to imagine scenes and events that exist outside of ourselves. To 'play through' and draw lessons from past events, possible future events, and even events that will never come into existence.

You spend your entire day swimming in a sea of stories. Imagine for a moment that we met up one afternoon for coffee. How would you answer the following questions?

- What do you do for a living?
- How did you get into that?
- How has your year to date been?
- How has your day been?

All these questions get answered with a story. It may be a mundane story about regular day-to-day happenings, but nonetheless each answer would be a story.

I see people telling stories and listening to stories, every time I step outside the house. Every time I go to the local pub, there are people telling stories. Every time I catch a tram, there are people telling (sometimes juicy) stories, albeit often through the medium of a mobile telephone.

Stories are like the fabric of life; our way of viewing the world. As you tell your stories you leave little fingerprints on that fabric. Each story you tell contains a microscopic slice of your experience as a person.

Real vs Non-Real events

As the picture-reels of your imagination roll in your head, your mind's eye is poor at distinguishing between real and non-real events. Even when you're asleep, a dream can still *feel* real. The fear you feel when you first wake up from a nightmare is a real physical response to something that has scared you.

When you're in the cinema watching a film, the emotions you feel are also real. If the story is good, we feel genuine fear when the hero of the story gets into danger. We feel real discomfort when they make poor decisions.

Neuroscientists have found[1] that when we watch somebody who is in pain, it activates the area of our own brain called the 'pain matrix'. In real time your brain runs a compelling simulation of what it would be like in the character's situation. This simulation is the basis of empathy; the ability to feel the emotions of others. To an extent you really do feel their pain.

The way we feel empathy may be more complicated than we realise. In a fascinating experiment, the neuroscientists showed two groups of people a shocking film, and measured activity the pain matrix area of the participants' brains. One group of participants consisted only of people who inject their facial muscles with the paralysis toxin Botox. The second group was made up of non-Botox users. The Botox users showed a lower level of pain in response to the film.

When we come face to face with another person, it seems we temporarily mirror the other person's facial expressions to help us read their emotions. It's almost like we 'try on' their facial expression, to see for ourselves how they are feeling. People with less control over their face may lose some capacity to feel empathy.

All of this helps to explain why a story, which we know not to be real, triggers the real emotional response we can feel. It helps to explain why we can cry at a film or television programme, even when the acting is less than exceptional. We feel an emotion because over the course of a story we build a connection with the hero. To a degree we end up walking in their shoes, trying on their emotions.

You don't choose whether you feel these emotions or not. Assuming your facial muscles are working correctly, it's an autonomic physiological response.

When you tell stories in your marketing, you're really building an emotional connection with your reader. You're building a connection so that when you need to ask them for something, you already have their trusting attention.

A well-told story can introduce the same trance-like state of attention that a dream can command. In the midst of a compelling story it's possible to forget the time, or that the potatoes are boiling over, or that the bath has gone cold.

Everybody must sell, in some capacity. Whether you are selling yourself, your products or your ideas, you can only transact a deal with someone if you have their attention. And attention has become increasingly hard to keep hold of.

You can get the attention of potential customers easily enough. You can post something attention-grabbing on Facebook, or Twitter. But keeping that attention beyond the initial interaction, or the initial 'like', has become difficult. If a customer is going to spend good money with you, they have to know, like and trust you. Building this trust requires an extended period of attention, not just a flash-in-the-pan Facebook post.

Storytelling is the best way to keep the attention of your audience over a long period of time. But why do stories generate this level of ongoing attention? Why are we so in-tune with stories?

Why do we seem to have a story-radar, blipping around in our minds?

[1]. See for example http://thescienceexplorer.com/brain-and-body/botox-inhibits-deep-emotions-and-ability-empathize (https://goo.gl/aHiqKQ)

More than mere 'Entertainment'

Over the last 200 years, storytelling has become synonymous with the word 'entertainment'. The most popular modern form of story is the film, or movie. Most people will tell you they go to the cinema to be *entertained*.

But is it really this simple?

Entertainment is one role of a story, and certainly an appealing role. But a story that only serves to entertain is quickly forgotten. After the bombs, explosions and special effects die down, you go back to 'real life' with the same outlook, perspective and experience. The entertainment quickly evaporates once the movie ends.

In his book *The Pledge*, Michael Masterson argues that all the activities you fill your life with fall into three categories; golden, vaporous and acidic.

Acidic activities are things that harm you, or harm your relationships with those around you. Vaporous activities leave you more or less the same. Golden activities improve you in some way.

A single activity can fall into all three categories, depending on the circumstances. For me, getting drunk is an acidic activity. I don't do it *very* often, but drunkenness usually leads to me being obnoxious and sick. (In that order).

In the vapour category, I'll sometimes have a small glass of whisky at home. The odd measure of whisky here and there leaves me as I was, but the pleasure I feel from drinking it evaporates quickly once the glass is empty.

Sharing a good whisky with a friend I haven't seen for a long time is a golden activity. The drinking itself is a catalyst to strengthen my relationships with those around me, which in a way improves me.

Using the same framework to look at entertainment, I would argue that playing video games is an acidic activity. Especially modern computer games, where it is possible to disappear into a fabricated world for weeks at a time, talking only to people you know online.

Most Hollywood movies belong in the vapour category. It's entertaining at the time; a bit like a mental joy-ride. But once the film ends and the ride stops, you're back to where you were before the film.

In the golden category, an exceptional film will both entertain you, and teach you something along the way. When you watch *The Shawshank Redemption*, or *Fatal Attraction*, the film is still entertaining. But underneath the entertainment the film has a deeper message. 'Watch yourself...' is the message. 'This *could happen to you...*'

Obviously the film heightens the message through drama. It's unlikely that in real life you would commit adultery with a woman who would go on to boil your daughter's pet rabbit. But we recognise a truth in the warning.

A great story entertains you, but is also does something else. It lingers around in a subconscious brain for a little while, poking and prodding at things you thought you knew.

The challenge we face as business owners, marketers and humans, is to tell more golden stories. To tell stories that still entertain your audience, but also leave them wiser and better informed.

You don't have to broadcast the fact that you are telling a story. You don't have to start off by saying 'once upon a time'. In the last couple of pages I've told you about my whisky drinking habits to illustrate the point I wanted to make. I could have just told you the point without the illustration, but it wouldn't have been as illuminating.

Most marketers shy away from telling stories, believing instead that their customers are only interested in information. It is true that the closer somebody comes to placing an order with you, the more information they need about your proposition. But to get to that point, you need to have held their attention for a period of time.

To my knowledge, stories are the most effective and least understood way to do this.

Storytelling was once an essential survival skill...

As a species, modern humans (*Homo sapiens*) are a relatively new addition to the world. Our ancestors first appeared in Africa, about 200,000 years ago. If this sounds like a long time to you, consider that the Tyrannosaurus Rex lived 65 million years ago.

In the long history of the Earth, human dominance is a relatively recent development. And human dominance, it seems, was once far from assured.

Most people who live outside of Africa can genetically trace their lineage back to a small group of humans who left Africa, about 100,000 years ago. Geneticists estimate there were no more than between 150 and 1000 individuals in the group.

At the time, leaving Africa would have been a major ordeal. As it does today, the Sahara desert presented an impassable barrier to the North. A widely-held belief is that our intrepid ancestors 'escaped' from Africa across the Red Sea, in a short window of opportunity when sea levels plummeted by up to 70 metres. We'll never know for sure, but it's likely they will have rafted part of the way across, in treacherous conditions.

On arriving in Arabia, they would have been confronted with more desert. How would they have survived on the arid Arabian

Peninsula? And how would they have escaped, to colonise the rest of the world?

The evidence may lie off the coast of Arabia, on the sea floor. With sea levels much lower, it's possible there were once a series of natural springs along the coast.

It's possible that over thousands of years, our ancestors made their way around the Arabian coast, stopping off at green centres of respite.

Regardless of whether the 'escape from Africa' theory is historically accurate; do you see how this already has the beginnings of an epic story? We already have a 'quest' plot on our hands. We have the 'helping' rejuvenating forces of the springs. We have the 'deadly force' of the desert, complete with any monsters it may have contained.

Even if the story isn't true, it's certainly plausible enough for your mind's eye to entertain the image, and for it to hold your attention. And stories hold your attention for an important reason.

Thousands of years ago, survival was more perilous than it is today. And yet, evidence suggests that early humans were all telling stories, to each other and to themselves. Storytelling was a core pillar of human survival, not a passive pastime for quiet periods.

When modern humans first entered Europe about 70,000 years ago, Europe was already occupied by another human species called Neanderthals. Neanderthals were bigger than us. They had bigger brains, and better tools. They were better adapted to the cold.

So why did modern humans survive, and Neanderthals die out?

A carved figure of a lion man was found in Eastern Europe, preserved in a bog. Experts believe it is 35,000 years old, and the work of a modern human.

Importantly, similar copies of the lion man have been found at sites 30-50 kilometres apart. That's a long way on foot.

Contrary to popular belief, the early tribes of modern humans were never isolated. Unlike Neanderthals, who lived in small isolated tribes, modern humans across fairly large areas seem to have shared an identity and culture through their art.

Art and storytelling today still holds the same purpose it did 35,000 years ago; to foster a shared understanding and identity. None of the great feats of human achievement have been accomplished by people working in isolation. Artistic expression and storytelling was an early technology that gave modern humans an advantage over competing species. It's possible we were simply better at collaborating through a shared culture; a culture nurtured by art, stories and rituals.

You can still see this binding cultural effect in indigenous cultures around the world. The totem poles of the native North Americans served the same purpose as the woven textiles of the Inca. They both served to bind members of the community together in a shared culture and identity.

Sometimes the stories are told in different formats; songs, dances, rituals, drawings.

The artefact above is called a khipu, which in the Inca language Quechua means 'knot'. It belonged to the Chachapoyans, a civilisation that thrived in Northern Peru before the Inca expansion.

Nobody knows what the khipu represents, but experts think it was ornamental, rather than an item of clothing. Each strand contains knots of different sizes, spaced at different intervals. Collectively we have now lost the ability to interpret the khipu, but it may represent a cultural history, or story.

In the history of human development, the written word is a relatively recent technology. For thousands of years, stories were the only way knowledge and cultural memories were passed on from one generation to the next. Stories would have been told verbally, or perhaps using devices like a khipu.

Storytelling rituals are just as important today as they were for ancient people. Every year on Remembrance Sunday, I am rightly told off by my wife when I forget to buy a poppy.

Remembrance Sunday is important because it passes on a shared cultural memory. As the final survivors of the two World Wars pass away, the story of the horror is all we have to learn from. It was George Orwell who said that the best way to destroy a people is to deny and obliterate their own understanding of their history.

The line between history and storytelling is blurry. A historical narrative must be maintained using stories, or else it fades away. The lessons must be passed to the next generation, and storytelling is *still* the most effective tool to do that.

When you consider the role that stories have played in human development, is it any wonder they do such a good job of holding your attention?

How do stories relate to your business?

The best theories about the way the world works are invariably simple. One of my favourite theories about business is Simon Sinek's *Golden Circle*.

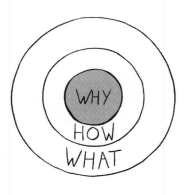

The 'what' circle represents everything that you *do*. It includes all your offers, features and benefits. Most business owners have a clear idea of what it is they do.

The 'how' circle is how you do it, your 'Unique Selling Proposition', or point of differentiation. Few businesses have a truly unique proposition, or way of doing things.

At the highest level, we have 'why'. Why includes why your business exists and what you believe in.

The obvious thing to do is to go from the outside in, to go from the clearest thing to the fuzziest. The real challenge in marketing your business is to tackle the fuzzy issue of why, and communicate this before you talk about how and what.

In the brain of your potential customer, the 'outer brain' or neocortex processes all rational 'what' arguments. The neocortex oversees rational thought, and can process complex information about features, benefits and pricing. Unfortunately however, the neocortex has no decision making authority. It can only serve to justify a decision with logic.

The neocortex is like a statistician tucked away in a government office. It can review the numbers. It can *recommend* a logical, sensible course of action. But it cannot make any decisions.

So where do the decisions happen?

Decisions themselves are made by the older part of your brain, the limbic system. The limbic system deals with emotions, feelings and social connections. It's where trust and loyalty come from, and it is responsible for every decision you ever make.

I recently watched a documentary about the human brain, which featured a lady called Tammy. Tammy had fallen off a motorcycle, and injured her head. The injury had somehow 'unlinked' emotion and logic in her brain. In the programme, Tammy and the film production team went into a supermarket.

In the store, all decisions for Tammy were a big deal. Tammy could take on information about six choices of apple, but she wasn't able to prioritise one option over another. She struggled to come to any decisions because her limbic system had somehow been disconnected from the decision-making process.

Your customers find it difficult to explain what goes on in their emotional decision making process. This is partly because they would rather you didn't know, but mainly because logical neocortex-level arguments are easier to articulate.

Nobody ever bought a MacBook because it was a better deal than a Windows-based PC. If you're a Mac user, you can justify your decision to me any way you like, but at some point your limbic brain emotionally bought into the idea of the Mac. Before people buy what you do, they first buy why you do it.

Storytelling allows you to move the conversation in your marketing away from *what* you do, towards the higher emotional levels of *how* and *why*. A story has the ability to slip past the logical gatekeeper in your prospect's brain, and first engage the limbic system with an emotionally compelling story.

If you want to tell an emotionally compelling story, an obvious place to start is your origin story. How did the business come into existence?

The origin story is one of the most captivating stories in human existence, seeking to address the eternal question, 'where did we come from?' At the heart of any worldview is a belief about your origins, and every great civilisation of the world has a founding story.

In Inca mythology, Manco Cápac and his brother Pacha Kamaq were said to have emerged from the waters of Lake Titicaca. In Roman mythology, Romulus and Remus were said to have been suckled by a wolf after they were abandoned on the Tiber river. The English were fascinated for centuries by the legend of King

Arthur, who is said to have led the defence of Britain against Saxon invaders in the 5th and 6th centuries.

Whether these stories contain any truth is besides the point. Each story served to bind together an otherwise disparate group of people, who would go on to build a great civilisation.

Your business has an origin story. It has stories that bind both employees and customers into your world. The stories you tell provide a shared culture that pull ideal customers towards your business.

When you're not a big player, like an Apple, Amazon or Google of this world, you have to tell your story if you want to stand out. You have to tell your story if you want potential customers to see your value, and see you as being different.

Your origin story is the first tool at your disposal to communicate *why* you do what you do, rather than *what* you do. Talking about what you do is not sufficient if you want people to spend good money with you.

The second tool at your disposal is to write about your beliefs. What are all the things you believe to be true about your business, or about your market? As a starting point, write out all the things you believe in which relate to your work. If you would like some inspiration you can read all of the things that I believe in at www.truestoryselling.com/beliefs.

Each belief becomes a potential story you can use in your marketing. Like origin stories, belief stories are another way to communicate *why* you do what you do.

The Commodity Caveat

The advice I am offering here applies best to companies who provide extraordinary value to their clients, but struggle to communicate exactly what that value is.

If you own or work for a business selling a 'known' commodity, like screws or nails, spending time communicating your *why* may be a poor use of your time. What you need instead is offers, sales and promotions. Thin margins and high volume becomes the name of the game. Personally, that isn't a game I'm interested in playing.

If you're not selling commodities at volume, you need to build an emotional connection with your customers by telling stories.

So, we've established why you should be using stories in your marketing. But what does a *good* story actually consist of?

What Makes a 'Good' Story?

1. The Hero Formula: Expert, Victim, Flaw

The first attribute of a good story is the 'hero formula'. You can have a great plot running through your story, but if your main character is boring the story will fall flat on its face.

I've taken the hero formula from film producer Joshua Russell, who argues that an intriguing, engaging story character must have three elements: expert, victim and flaw.

First, they must be an expert in something. They must have skills in something. They must have something they are good at, even if the thing they are good at is not immediately obvious to either themselves or us.

Batman is an expert at fighting crime. Dexter is an expert blood spatter analyst. Jane Eyre has the strength of character to rebel against her aunt and cousins, and tell them exactly what she thinks of them. In *The Lion King*, Simba is a young and powerful lion.

Second, they must be a victim in some way. Batman, Dexter and

Jane Eyre are all orphans. In literature, killing off one or both parents is perhaps the easiest way to victimise the hero of the story. Most of the main Disney characters are orphans, or at least have one parent missing. This victimisation is essential because it creates a sense of injustice. It hints at the encroachment of some dark power.

Killing off one or both parents also hints at a deeper, more fundamental role of storytelling, because it throws the main character out of balance. With one or both parents absent they become egocentric, or confused about who they really are. Often they will behave with a lack of empathy and understanding. The victim event creates a hole in the character's make up, and the story is really about how this hole gets filled, and how balance is redressed.

We're all victims of circumstance at some point in our lives. Subconsciously we all make some decisions based on old emotional wounds. Perhaps the 'victim event' wasn't the death of a parent, but the time you were overlooked for a role in a school play. Perhaps it was the time you were bullied in infant school.

We all have something like this in our past, and it contributes to who we are. The character in a story has to be a victim in some way, or else they aren't really human. Even in shows like *The X Factor*, many successful acts have a victim event in their back-story.

Victimising the main character also plays a role in the third part of the formula; flaw.

Batman is flawed because he has to hide his identity and operate behind a mask. Dexter's flaw is his 'dark passenger', which compels him to kill. Jane Eyre's flaw is she cannot see people for who they really are. Simba's flaw is that he cannot see who he really is.

Like victim events, flaws are a real, everyday part of human existence. We all have flaws of our own, and we recognise these in the flaws of the hero.

A character's flaw allows us as the audience to connect to the character on an emotional level. We don't respond to our own flaws in the same way as the hero. We don't run around in the night murdering people, like Dexter does. But we recognise that he is responding to a flaw in his character created by the death of his parents. Dexter uses murder as a form of imitation love, in the absence of real love from an absent maternal figure. To a degree, we see some echo of our own lives in the psychological make-up of the hero.

The flaws in the hero's character mean they can never achieve the objective of the story by working alone. They have to interact with other characters in the plot to achieve their objective. Batman must work with Robin to defeat the Riddler. Simba must be given perspective by Nala and Rafiki, before he can challenge Scar. Most stories have 'good' helper characters, who enable the hero to grow or change into his true self.

This brings us back to the origins of storytelling, where stories served to bind people together in a shared culture, to achieve bigger objectives than are possible alone. One of the implicit lessons of storytelling is that we rarely achieve our goals by working in isolation.

Nowhere is this more apparent than in the tragedy plot.

One of the defining features of tragedy is the hero always becomes more and more isolated throughout the story. Unlike in a comedy where social connections are slowly repaired, a tragic hero always ends up isolated and alone. A tragic hero will usually start off well connected, before murdering or shunning those around him throughout the story.

Dexter ends up alone and isolated, having murdered or pushed away those around him. Macbeth ends up isolated in insanity. King Lear ends up in isolated madness, cut off from his 'light' daughter Cordelia.

A truly engaging character must have deep-rooted psychological problems, perhaps stemming from previous victim events. The point of the story is then to show how the character engages with those around him, and grows as a person to overcome his flaws. As we'll see, in the tragedy plot this never quite happens, although the outcome of the story is still the same.

A good story exposes the main characters in a vulnerable way. It's this vulnerability that allows you to see them for who they really are, and emotionally connect with them.

What 'Expert, Victim, Flaw' means for you

There are plenty of literary examples of vulnerable characters, who display obvious victim events and flaws. But how about real-life business examples?

Most business owners wake up in the morning and strap on their flawless 'business armour'. Rather than go out into the world as their real 'flawed' selves, they go out as a flawless persona of themselves.

If you own or work in a personality-based business, where the brand is based around the personality of a single person or character, you need to pay close attention to the expert, victim, flaw formula. If you're the face of your business, you should expose your flaws just as much as your expertise.

We're all an expert in something. We've all been a victim of circumstance at some point in our lives. And sometimes as a consequence of being a victim, we all have flaws.

Victim and flaw are often interwoven. Sometimes there will be a single event in your past which caused you to think a certain way, or behave a certain way.

If there isn't an obvious 'victim event' in your past, your flaws can still show up in subtle recurring behaviours.

Take me for example. If you delve into my past I'm not an obvious victim in any way. I had a fairly uneventful childhood. I was a reasonably good student. I don't recall anything exceptionally bad happening. No major family traumas. No major run-ins with the authorities.

I do however have flaws, and they play out in my life in subtle ways.

One way to identify your flaws is to look at your hobbies. My main hobbies are archery, running and writing. All three are individual activities. Yes, you can shoot or run as part of a team. But the act itself of running, or shooting an arrow, is an introspective private affair. By contrast I hate playing team games, like rugby or football.

In the sports I do, I care little for medals and classifications. I was shooting at a competition recently where I had the highest handicap of any archer, because I hardly ever submit any scores. As an archer, I basically want to be left alone so I can get on with my shooting in a private, introspective way.

This behaviour shows up in my business life too. I force myself to look at my business numbers. But I don't *really* care about the numbers. Not unless they're particularly bad.

I can set targets for myself, but I don't care whether I hit them (even when there is a significant financial impact). I would be impossible to motivate as a sales person. Most of the time I just want to be left alone to do my thing.

I've tried to fix this personal flaw, and I can't. The only answer is to surround myself with people who *like* numbers, targets and spreadsheets, which then brings other characters into my story.

Flaws and strengths are two sides of the same coin. You cannot be an expert in something without also being flawed at something else. My flaw for numbers and targets is counterbalanced by the introspection I think I bring to my writing.

My flaw is that I tend to isolate myself, in my hobbies and in my work. At the same time that hints at a strength, in that I have always been an independent thinker, willing to go against the grain even at financial expense. I've always been willing to stand up for what I believe in.

If you subscribe to my daily emails you'll find that I write about my flaws a lot. Not in an especially negative way, but in a way that allows you to know the real me.

Another way to dig out your flaws is to think about all the things you got in trouble for at school. I was never in trouble much at school, but I remember standing nervously outside the deputy head's office when I was doing my A-levels.

On Tuesdays, a friend and I had 'free periods' in between break and lunch. Which meant we were 'free' between 11AM and 1.45PM. You were supposed to stay in school during that time, supposedly to study.

Our version of 'studying' was to dodge out of school at 11AM, and head to a local snooker hall. To study the art of playing snooker, you understand.

One Tuesday we were playing snooker when my phone rang.

"There's been a fire alarm," said the caller, darkly. "And Mr. Askew wants to know where you are..."

A day later I stood outside deputy head Askew's office. I had nothing to say to him, other than I had 'felt ill' and had gone home, apparently without telling anyone or signing out. Telling him the truth would have given the game away.

He nailed me of course, on the principle that in a genuine fire a fire fighter would be sent back into the building to look for people missing. I couldn't argue with that, but I still wasn't willing to sacrifice our snooker sessions.

Do you see a pattern emerging here? Even at school I was prone to slip away from what everyone else was doing and do my own thing. My work has since followed the same pattern. I abandoned my last two office jobs for unknown self-employment.

One of my earliest memories at infant school is of a task we were given to make Easter cards. I was perhaps five or six years old. I came up with a plan for an elaborate musical card, powered by AA batteries. I came nowhere near to finishing the card, barely designing the front cover.

"I think you've been a little ambitious," was the teacher's semi-friendly remark.

I still see this behaviour playing out today in different ways. I'm better now at selecting projects that are within my capabilities, but once a project is complete I'll often drop it in favour of a new one. The Confusion Clinic marketing archive is full of half-finished or rarely promoted special reports.

The same flaws in my character keep recurring over and over in my behaviour. Your flaws can also be your strengths, if you embrace them in the right way and surround yourself with the right people.

If you want to build up a credible character in your marketing, whether or not that character is you, **you have to expose their flaws**.

Most business stories focus exclusively on the 'expert' part of the expert, victim, flaw equation. To most people writing about your flaws makes you appear weak, or imperfect. Most people assume this would put a potential customer off.

I've spent the last few pages telling you about my flaws, and I'm willing to bet you haven't yet thrown down the book in disgust. If anything, you now know the real me a little better. Telling you about my flaws also hints at my strengths.

Exposing your flaws may put *some* potential customers off, but in general those aren't the customers you want to work with. What it *does* do is expose your real self, and allows you to be vulnerable. It is vulnerability that allows people to connect with you on an emotional, limbic-brain, decision-making level.

2. A focused plot, but detailed episodes

The second aspect to a great story is a focused plot and detailed episodes. You should be able to summarise the plot of your story in a few sentences, even if the action itself plays out over many pages.

Take the Odyssey, for example. The Odyssey is an epic poem, written by the Greek poet Homer around 800BC. It runs for hundreds of pages, but the plot can be summarised as follows.

After fighting a great battle, a man (Odysseus) is away from home for many years. His efforts to return home are held up by various dark powers, including Odysseus' envious arch enemy, Poseidon. Meanwhile at home, suitors are chasing Odysseus' wife and plotting against his son. Eventually, almost defeated, he arrives home. He attacks and kills the suitors, and reclaims what is rightfully his.

That's all you need to know about the plot. Everything else is episode.

It is easier to see the distinction between plot and episodes by looking at a television series, where the action is actually is split into episodes. The plot of *Breaking Bad* can be summarised as follows.

A man on the verge of death discovers he can earn money by producing crystal meth. His ego becomes blinded by the new-found wealth. To keep his new life hidden, he slowly kills the relationships with the people around him, becoming more and more isolated. He ends up completely isolated and desolate, finally sacrificing himself to rescue his former business partner.

That's the plot. The episodes ebb and flow like a seemingly never-ending river, but the plot itself is relatively simple.

One of the most common mistakes I see people making when they start to use stories in their marketing is to tell a story that has dual focus. You end up writing a story that is about something, but then about something else.

Lord of the Rings is an example of a dual-focus plot. Initially the story is about Frodo, but eventually the main character of the story turns out to be Aragorn. It's like Tolkien set out to write a children's story about hobbits, and part-way through realised he needed a more adult hero. The story ends up being about both, to the detriment of the plot.

The stories you tell should be singular in plot focus, and told fully to completion. If you think the story is getting too long, split it out into multiple episodes, instalments or emails.

3. An archetypal story pattern

The third element of a great evergreen story is the presence of at least one archetypal plot.

So, what is an 'archetypal plot'?

When I was at school I studied English Literature at A-level. I distinctly remember other friends ridiculing this choice.

"You're doing an A-level in *reading books...*" they would inform me, mockingly.

I could feel at the time that reading and studying literature was important. I could sense the depth of the subject; that there was an important undercurrent running under the surface. But I couldn't quite see what it was.

When you study English Literature, you are taught to look for patterns in a story. The patterns always seemed obvious to me when they were pointed out. Once it had been pointed out, it was obvious to me that Blanche DuBois had to either die at the end of *A Streetcar Named Desire*, or go to an asylum. In my head I was like 'well... they weren't exactly going to live *happily ever after*, were they?'

It was obvious to me that there were recurring patterns in the stories we studied, but identifying the patterns for myself always seemed a step too far.

For a number of years, I listened to people in the copywriting world talk about the so-called 'hero's journey'. The hero's journey is the idea that there is a single 'master story' that dictates both our lives, and the stories we consume.

Every story has a hero or heroine (or possibly both), around who the plot revolves. The 'hero's journey' hints at a fundamental role of storytelling, where a story is always about a before and after state in the hero's fortunes. Every story has a starting point and an end point, and the point of the story is the drama of the journey in the middle.

I could see a fundamental truth in the hero's journey, but to me it seemed too broad-brush to be practically useful. I struggled to see how the hero's journey could be useful to me when I was writing an email to my customer list, for example.

Early in 2016, a friend recommended I pick up a copy of Christopher Booker's book *The Seven Basic Plots*. Just like I had always dismissed the 'hero's journey' as being too simplistic, I had always rejected the idea that the stories of the world could be categorised by a number of 'basic plots'. Surely, I thought, this was another over-optimistic myth of categorisation?

In a book that took 30 years to write, Booker analyses hundreds of novels, poems, plays and films. He classifies the stories into seven 'archetypal' plots. An archetypal plot is a plot pattern that has emerged in countless stories across different times and cultures, because it reveals some kind of universal truth about human nature.

Booker argues for example that the *Epic of Gilgamesh*, written 4000 years ago in ancient Mesopotamia (now Iraq), has an almost identical storyline to the movie *Jaws*. He calls this plot 'overcoming the monster'.

The opposite of an archetypal story is a stereotypical story. The Sherlock Holmes stories would not be as interesting to the inhabitants of ancient Babylon as they are to modern Londoners, hence the story is based around a stereotype. Stereotypical stories are easier to write, but are only interesting to readers in a particular time and culture.

As I read through *The Seven Basic Plots*, it struck me that Booker may indeed be onto something. All of the seven plots he identifies follow the same overall pattern, which hints that they all describe the elusive hero's journey in some way. What each plot provides is a clear plot template we can use, complete with a pre-populated cast of characters. Every 'quest' plot has 'helper' characters, like Sam, Merry and Pippin in *Lord of the Rings*. Every 'tragedy' plot has a tempter or temptress, like Lady Macbeth in *Macbeth*.

All of Booker's seven plots describe the same archetypal story, the hero's journey. But like a good photographer, they all do so from different angles and perspectives. Underlying story flow behind each of the plots looks like this:

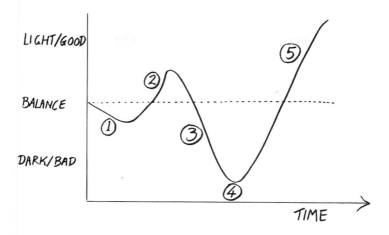

Broadly speaking, all archetypal plots have five phases:

1. Anticipation, or 'call'

At the anticipation stage, we are presented with an opening situation. In *The Lord of the Rings*, we are introduced to Frodo and the hobbits, living happily in The Shire. *The Lion King* starts off with the kingdom functioning in equilibrium, with Simba supported by both his parents; Mufasa and Sarabi.

Very quickly however, a dark force encroaches onto the story. In *The Lion King*, Mufasa is killed by Scar. In *The Lord of the Rings*, dark riders arrive in The Shire. Stage 1 is called 'the call' because it is no longer possible for the hero of the story to continue their previous path. Some force of darkness has encroached onto the happy equilibrium of the world, if indeed there was one to begin with.

At the anticipation stage the hero's current situation becomes untenable, and some course of action must be taken.

2. The dream stage

In the 'dream' stage, things seem to be going well for our hero. The hobbits make good progress towards Mordor. In *The Jungle Book*, Mowgli gets most of the way back to the man-village. Macbeth looks like he will get away with the murder of King Duncan.

3. The frustration stage

In the frustration stage, the full extent of the 'dark power' finally becomes apparent. The full power of Mordor is finally revealed. Scar's tyrannical regime destroys all life in the kingdom. Mowgli runs away from the man-village, back into the clutches of Shere Khan.

Something we see at the frustration stage is a constriction and expansion of the plot. A constriction happens when the dark force in the story exerts pressure on the hero. An expansion happens when pressure is released, allowing the hero to make progress towards the goal of the story. The constrictions and expansions escalate until we get to stage 4, the climax.

4. The climax

At the climax, there will be a final confrontation between good and bad forces in the story. At this point the dark force in the story exerts maximum pressure on the hero. It will seem for a while like the dark forces are almost certain to succeed.

All dark forces however have a weakness, or Achilles' heel, because they are always out of balance. Dark characters are usually selfish, driven by egotistical desires. Their chief pursuit is their own power, control and happiness, usually at the expense of everything else.

This selfishness also makes them weak. To a degree, they are blind to the true nature of the situation, or to the true identity of the hero. This blindness is always the source of their downfall.

5. The resolution

In stage 5, the dark force is defeated or repelled. Things either go back to how they were, or more often than not *better* than how they were. Balance and order return to the kingdom. Our hero, who has now discovered his true identity, is appropriately rewarded. Often this means a 'happy union' with the true heroine of the story. The outcome of the story is a renewal of life and purpose.

Even in a tragedy, the plot pattern is still the same. Macbeth is defeated, and order finally returns to the kingdom of Scotland. The tragic hero is destroyed, but a renewal of life is still the eventual outcome.

What the five-phases describe is a move from beginning, to middle, to end. Joshua Russell calls this the 'subject, revision, new subject' pattern. You start off in the beginning with an opening situation, or subject. That situation is revised in the middle of the story, finishing with a new subject at the end.

If you consider the five phases of an archetypal plot, stage 1 is the initial subject matter, or beginning. Stages 2 – 4 are the revision, with all the ups and downs the revision contains. The bigger and more dramatic the ups and downs, the more exciting the story becomes. Stage 5 is the new subject, or end of the story.

When you write a story in a marketing email, you'll generally start off by explaining the context of the story. This is the beginning, or first subject. You'll then have some kind of conflict or 'revision' in the middle, with a handful of 'ups' and 'downs'. And you'll finish on the outcome of the story, which is the new subject.

We'll look at exactly how to do this in Part 2.

Part 2: The 7-Step Production Process

You now understand why stories are such an effective tool of persuasion, and why stories permeate every aspect of society. But how do you write effective stories *quickly*? Speed of production is everything. The perfect story that takes four weeks to write will do little to increase your sales.

This section of the book shares how to write story-based emails in hours, rather than weeks. I've focused on email in this section because email is probably a technology you already have at your disposal.

You could just as easily follow the steps to create stories in other media. Some of my students have used the seven steps to create stories for webinar presentations, video scripts and sales meetings.

Think about email first, but keep an eye open for opportunities to apply these techniques in other media.

Why open your email with a story?

After the headline, the most important part of any piece of persuasive writing is the *lead*. The lead is the first few sentences, or opening idea.

In *Great Leads: The Six Easiest Ways to Start Any Sales Message*, John Forde and Michael Masterson pick apart a collection of great sales letters to determine what makes a great lead. They identified six types of lead, falling on a scale.

At the one end of the scale, you can lead with your offer. If your prospects are highly familiar with your products and services it can be best to immediately lead with pricing and promotion details.

At the other end of the scale, you can lead with a story. The story makes no direct mention of the offer, but engages the reader and leads them towards the call to action.

Most of my emails follow this format, where the story portion of the email comes first. I call this the 'open sandwich' format.

An 'open sandwich' is a sandwich without the top layer of bread. As your reader bites into the sandwich they first get to the filling, which is the story.

The story in an 'open sandwich' email goes at the beginning, with your content coming at the end. The content is the information you want to communicate to your reader about your features, your benefits and your offers. The content makes up the bread portion of the sandwich.

When most companies send marketing emails they completely skip the story part of the email, and only write about content. Asking people to read emails without any sort of story is like asking them to eat dry bread. They might eat your dry bread once or twice, but they will quickly tire of it. If you want to communicate with your customers over months and years, you need to be telling stories.

The story in your email acts as bait. When an email arrives, you first look at the sender's name and decide whether you are going to read the email now, later or not at all. If the email is from a marketing firm, you may skip it all together. If the email is from a colleague, you may read it later. If the email is from a client who owes you money, you'll probably open it straight away.

If you decide to open the email you'll then look at the subject line, and possibly the opening sentence. If the subject line and opening sentence look interesting or intriguing, you'll read a little further.

Good stories act as bait, and keep people reading. The job of a story is to lead the reader into your content. You can have the best content in the world, but if nobody reads it no good will come of it.

At the point where your story ends and your content begins, we have something called 'the reconnect'. The reconnect is like the margarine of the sandwich, glueing story and content together.

Beginners often think that a story must directly relate to the content, but this isn't the case. What matters is the way the story *connects* to the content. The art of story selection becomes less to do with selecting the 'perfect story', and more to do with selecting a variety of stories your audience will relate to.

My favourite sandwich filling is roast pork. An odd choice, you might argue, for somebody who rarely eats meat. One of the benefits of living in Sheffield is that roast pork sandwiches are taken seriously here. Your standard pork sandwich includes a generous serving of pork, apple sauce and crackling. Some places will also put dripping on the sandwich if you ask.

As a one-off, a pork sandwich is probably the best sandwich for grabbing my attention. Variation however is also required. As much as I love roast pork sandwiches, I cannot eat one every day. It would be bad for my health, and I would burn in vegetarian hell.

Your stories must be varied if you are to maintain interest over a long period of time, and varying your stories is akin to varying your sandwich fillings. Most marketers lack sufficient variety in their storytelling.

Just as bread varies between different sandwiches, the content in your emails will also vary. Some sandwiches come with big, thick slices of bread. In other sandwiches the bread is simply a medium to hold the filling.

And so it is with marketing emails. Some emails will contain a lengthy piece of content about your offer or call to action. Some may be thinner, perhaps only mentioning the next step in passing. Others may have no overt call to action at all, but will lay the groundwork for a later call to action.

The Importance of Process

I had tried in the past to create a process for writing story-based marketing emails, and every time I failed. I knew there *was* a process, but I thought it was too complicated to explain, with too many moving parts.

I thought this right up to December 2015. In December 2015 I attended a storytelling workshop in Amsterdam, run by Sean D'Souza (www.psychotactics.com). Most of the attendees were writers, in some capacity. Some of us were copywriters. Some of us were authors.

It became obvious to me that Sean had arrived with a process he was able to teach, and that it wouldn't have mattered if we had all shown up as mathematicians. We would all have stumbled in the same places, and made the same mistakes. After three days we all emerged from the course with the same skills.

This experience impacted me greatly. I already knew the importance of storytelling in communicating your uniqueness, but suddenly there was a model I could use to explain it to other people.

When I got home I expanded on Sean's process and added some thoughts of my own. I decided the best way to work through the process was to teach it to people. I set out a programme for a seven-week course. Three students signed up for the course, and together we began to work through the process I had produced.

For four hours a week we would work through the different storytelling steps. At the end of the third week we had completed the 'timeline technique', and I said "right… off you go! Take your timeline and write me a story."

After five minutes, it became clear that everybody was floundering. Suddenly the 'step by step' process I had produced didn't seem quite so 'step by step' any more.

It took me a few days to discover the answer.

I was on Instagram that weekend, scrolling through my newsfeed. Somebody I follow had posted a mind map of a talk Brené Brown had given. Brené is a researcher turned storyteller, and has given high-level talks on the importance of vulnerability.

The part of the mind map that caught my attention was a small note saying 'Shitty First Draft: Write It Down'. It struck me that this was a critical and missing step in my own writing process. It was a step that I was somewhat blind to, because as a writer I don't struggle getting my first drafts onto paper.

As I worked through this process with more clients I discovered that getting a first draft onto paper is a BIG deal.

The following week I added an additional step to the process called the Speedy First Draft. The Speedy First Draft allowed us to reduce the intimidation. Instead of trying to draft out an entire email in one go, my students were now taking a smaller, less scary step on the road to a finished email.

Small, less-scary steps lead to a higher number of completed emails. By following a series of do-able steps you no longer **need** to hire a copywriter, if you don't want to. If you have the knowledge, stories and time, it is possible to produce compelling story-based emails without relying on the 'black magic' of a copywriter.

Suddenly you're doing your own black magic; or at least that's what it looks like to everyone else. To everyone else you are writing engaging story-based emails at a frequency most people think impossible. To you, or to whoever on your team ends up in the copywriting role, you are simply following a structured step-by-step procedure.

Contrary to what many copywriters will tell you, the storytelling process isn't mysterious black magic. You may never write copy as well as a professional copywriter, but you may produce copy that delivers similar results. Your audience want to engage with **you** more than they want to critique your choice of words. If your stories are good and your information is good you'll generate results.

The Seven Step Formula

If you think back to the 'open sandwich' format, the seven steps described in this section only look at the story portion of your email. We're only looking at the sandwich filling here, or the 'lead'.

Most of my students have no problem telling me about the features and benefits of their products. I would trust that your content, the bread of your sandwich, is probably good. Usually it is the story section of the email that needs work.

The problem with opening an email with a story is the possibilities are unlimited. There are an unlimited range of stories you could tell in an unlimited number of ways. Such choice is hugely intimidating, so to begin with it helps to limit your choices to a series of sequential steps.

When you think about it, the way we learn any complicated skill is to break it down into steps.

Take archery for example. I am an archer, and shoot longbow at weekends. When you first take up archery the process of shooting an arrow is described as a set of distinct phases.

After a while, you realise that the process of shooting an arrow is more dynamic than the step-by-step approach you were initially taught. You realise that shooting an arrow is more like hitting a golf ball, with multiple variables and moving parts. You don't actually stay still on any particular step – it's a complex fluid motion.

But importantly you don't **start** with the golf ball analogy. If I told a beginner that shooting an arrow was like hitting a golf ball and they should just 'have at it', the results would be disastrous. You start with the step-by-step approach, by mastering one doable step at a time.

Eventually, with enough practice, you transcend the steps. The steps become so familiar that you do them without thinking. This is how true mastery works.

Rather like shooting an arrow, the process of writing a story for a marketing email can also be broken down into a series of steps.

The seven steps are:

1. Story selection
2. Create the timeline
3. Create the 'Speedy First Draft'
4. Create the Second Draft
5. Add suspense or intrigue
6. Reconnect to content
7. Editing

When you are learning to write better emails, the seven steps must happen **in order**. As tempting as it may seem, you should never write the first draft before creating the timeline. You should never start editing until you have completed the other six steps. The steps are a mental checklist to be completed **sequentially**.

Eventually as the process becomes ingrained you stop relying on the steps so much. If you follow my process step by step it is perfectly normal to adapt and modify steps later on as you become more experienced. You start off being taught my version of the process, and eventually end up with your own process. I actively encourage my students to do this.

You never completely abandon the steps once you master the process. The steps are always there to fall back on if things go wrong. When you get stuck you can always go back to beginner-mode, and revisit the seven steps. It will prop you up in times of need.

The point of following a mental checklist is you're no longer thinking about the intimidating prospect of writing a compelling story-based marketing email. Instead, you're only focused on the next step in the process.

I am not by any stretch claiming that I have the 'one best way' to write a nurture email. Far from it. What I am claiming is that I have a systematic step-by-step **starting point** that anyone can follow, even if you don't currently consider yourself to be a writer.

Step 0: Research

"Step zero?" I hear you cry. "But I thought there were only seven steps?"

There are only seven steps, once you know what you are going to write about.

Everybody seems to think the answer to their business communications problems is *better writing*. I see people going on copywriting courses to learn about headlines, bullets and benefits. They complete the course… and they *still don't know what to write about!*

When you include stories in your marketing you cannot wait until you are writing the email to start digging around for an appropriate story. The story must be ready to go ahead of time in a searchable, retrievable format.

My mind is like a giant sieve. New story ideas pop up all the time, but unless they are captured and stored they quickly fall through into the mental abyss. Most of my story ideas come at inopportune times, such as when I am sleeping, running or showering. I now go running with my mobile phone just so I can make a note of any ideas that come to me.

If you don't store an idea immediately it will evaporate into the atmosphere. I use a cloud-based storage tool called Evernote to store my ideas. Some of my more graphically-minded students also use Pinterest.

In Evernote, content you save is stored in 'notebooks'. I organise my Evernote notebooks into story research, content research and journal entries. Keeping a journal is a great way to generate story ideas for emails. The problem with a conventional journal is that searching and retrieving journal entries later can be difficult. Using Evernote solves this problem by making the text of my journal entries searchable. I can also create journal entries on my phone, using the Evernote app.

My story research notebook in Evernote contains clippings of anything I have found interesting. Emails, articles, images and social media posts can all end up in Evernote. Many of my ideas come from documentaries. I watch these on my phone with the subtitles turned on, and take screenshots of interesting things that I may use in the future as a story. The screenshot will then be saved in Evernote, along with brief notes and a tag to remind me what the story is about.

You can see an example at http://goo.gl/pYtfjm.

In Evernote, I've tagged this entry in as being about 'technology' and 'collaboration'. The tagging process is important, because tags help you to retrieve articles later on. If you had to summarise the item you are storing with a single word or phrase, what word would that be? That word will then become your tag.

You can tag an article as being about multiple things. An article could for example be about bravery, strength and leadership at the same time. If you feel that is the case then apply three tags.

The third Evernote notebook is content research. Content research covers anything you might want to include in the content section of the email. My content notebook is mostly made up of online articles, saved emails and photographs of book pages. Evernote can search text in an image, so you can add a photo of a book page and Evernote can then search the text later on.

Step 1: Story Selection

Once you have a growing store of things to write about you need to select a story. It is perhaps instructive to start our tour of story selection by looking at how *not* to select stories.

Hector Berlioz was a French composer of what we now call classical music. Berlioz was known for having a variety of love interests. In 1831 during a stay in Rome, Berlioz received communication that one of his mistresses at home was seeing another man.

In a fit of rage, Berlioz boarded a train bound for Paris disguised as a women. Berlioz was armed with a pistol and a phial of poison. His plan was to use his disguise to gain entry to his mistresses' home, shoot her and her new beau, and poison himself afterwards.

By the time the train had reached Nice, Berlioz had a change of heart, abandoning his plan to compose a love sonata instead. 'Rock and roll' behaviour is apparently nothing new.

Berlioz's most famous piece of music is the Symphonie Fantastique (1830). After attending a performance of Hamlet in 1827, Berlioz fell desperately in love with the Irish actress Harriet Smithson, who had played Ophelia. Berlioz bombarded her with love letters, to the point of stalking her.

Symphonie Fantastique is an expression of his pain at her rejection. To make it absolutely clear the piece was about Harriet

Smithson, Berlioz published extensive programme notes explaining exactly what each movement is meant to portray. The piece ends with 'the artist', as Berlioz refers to himself in the notes, killing himself in an opium overdose.

Symphonie Fantastique in my opinion is an expression of self-absorption. It worked for Berlioz though; Harriet Smithson attended the performance, studied the programme notes, and miraculously fell in love with Berlioz. They married in 1833, without Berlioz speaking a word of English, or Smithson a word of French.

Every time I listen to Berlioz's music I hear a sound that drips with self-indulgence. Berlioz had no interest at all in you as the listener. Berlioz's only interest was himself.

Most people write stories in the same way that Hector Berlioz wrote music; by focusing exclusively on themselves.

Yes, you can and should use personal stories in your emails. But you also need to remember that nobody is as interested in your life as you are.

I see many people writing daily emails, and writing about pretty mundane events. If you were making porridge this morning and ran out of milk I don't particularly want to hear about it, even if you do successfully link the story to your content.

The danger with including a mundane story is you run the risk of communicating without nurturing. You end up communicating for the sake of communicating without delivering value.

I'm not against telling stories that describe routine, everyday events, but you need to tell the story in a way that makes someone stop what they are doing and take note. The only way to do this is to consider me as the reader before you select your story.

The first measure of a story is to determine whether your

audience will be immediately familiar with your story. If you're in the United States and sell to an international audience, then writing endless stories about your son's American football exploits isn't going to resonate.

If you're in England and sell to a mostly American audience, then writing endless stories about British politics isn't going to work.

It sounds obvious, but most people never stop to think about this.

You don't have to select stories that people are intimately familiar with; just stories they will recognise without much explanation.

Take the Hector Berlioz story. To begin with you probably didn't notice I was telling you a story. The story should fly in under the radar without drawing too much attention to itself.

I selected the story because it was both unexpected and familiar. You may never have heard of Hector Berlioz, but you know what classical music is, and you know what a composer is. You also know what 'rock and roll' behaviour is, and may have smiled at Berlioz's antics.

I call this the 'Story Selection See-saw'. The mid-point in the see-saw is to select stories that illustrate your point, that are broadly familiar, and also completely unexpected. The stories you tell do not have to be *your* stories. I like to use personal stories, but if you only ever use personal stories you aren't varying up your sandwich fillings enough. I didn't come up with the Berlioz story. I found it and adapted it to my content.

Step 2: The Timeline

Once you have decided what story to use, you need to map it out visually. The best way to do this is to draw a timeline.

When I am drawing a timeline I will normally use a folded sheet of A4 paper, but you could also use a napkin, post-it note, or whatever else comes to hand. I find a folded sheet of A4 provides enough space to note six or seven story elements, which is about as many as you have space to include in a marketing email.

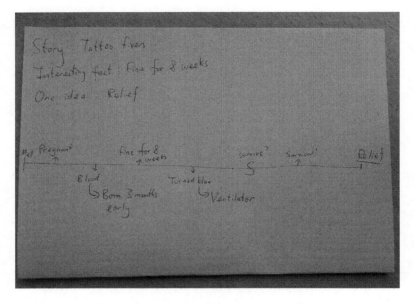

(Full size colour image: https://goo.gl/6bgfgQ)

First, make a note of the story in the top left. Underneath the story name make a note of the one idea. The one idea is the single word or phrase you believe the story to be about. If you think back to the research phase, the 'one idea' will usually be one of your Evernote tags.

Your one idea should ideally be a universal concept, rather than an item or name. Good examples of one ideas include fear, envy, bravery, strength, singularity, choices, dilemma, speed, efficiency, stupidity, mistakes, commitment.

When I first created this process one my students tried to use 'spring' (as in the season) as her one idea.

"What is it about spring that you want to talk about?" I asked.

"The changing seasons," she said. "New growth."

Growth became the one idea.

If you find yourself wanting to use a noun as a one idea, ask yourself what is it about that thing that you want to communicate?

If you are struggling to come up with a one idea for your story, it can also help to make a note of an interesting fact about the story. You don't have to note down an interesting fact, but often the interesting fact is a good interim step in identifying your one idea.

Let's say that I wanted to tell you a story about my run this afternoon. Many afternoons I go for a short run, usually to a local park. At first glance it might seem difficult to pull a one idea from such an unremarkable story.

If I also told you that I ran around the park barefoot, would you find it easier to come up with a one idea? The fact that I ran barefoot was the interesting fact. The interesting fact provides an angle from which you can extract your one idea.

Personally, my one idea based on that interesting fact would be 'connection'.

This raises an important point. I might peg the one idea as being about connection. You might peg the one idea as being about simplicity. Both are equally correct – there are no right and wrong answers.

The one idea is important because it marks the end of your story. Later, we'll then use the one idea to link your story to your content.

Once you have identified a one idea the next step is to note the main points of the story onto the timeline as 'ups' and 'downs'. Broadly speaking an 'up' is when something good happens, and a 'down' is where something bad happens.

The ups and the downs map the major ebbs and flow of the story. If you are writing a story for an email, you usually don't want to go above seven ups and downs. Beyond seven you will often find the story becomes too long. Sticking to fewer ups and downs forces you to select only the most important events to include in the story.

Mapping your story in this way allows you to visually see the flow of the story. Interesting stories always have a combination of ups and downs.

Imagine that you are at the cinema to see a movie. You sit down in your seat, equipped with a bucket of popcorn. The subject of the movie is a young lady from London.

Our young lady goes through school scoring straight A's. She enters a prestigious university. Out of university she makes time to travel the world, while at the same time lining up a lucrative graduate job. Three years into the graduate job she lands a job in senior management. Later that year she gets married, has a baby, and moves into her dream house...

Do you see the problem here? It's boring! It's all ups and no downs. Where's the crisis? Where's the calamity?

Let's say the exact same story came with a twist. When our young lady went travelling she was kidnapped in Peru and held hostage. While being held in captivity she became pregnant at the hands of her captors. When she eventually returned to England the graduate job opportunity had disappeared. She had to fight her way to success, starting her own business.

Which version of the story do you want to hear more of? The version where only good things happen? Or the version with the kidnapping?

A good story always has 'ups' and 'downs'. Good things happen, bad things happen. If your story is boring the contrast between the highs and lows probably is not pronounced enough.

One of my favourite films is the Jungle Book (the 1967 film, not the more recent film). If you want to spot ups and downs in a story you can do worse than to look at children's stories. The ups and the downs are often more pronounced, with the downs accompanied by nasty characters, dark clouds and inclement weather.

'Ups' and 'downs' in different forms are present in every area of your life when you start to look for them. Often the 'ups' aren't necessarily up and the 'downs' aren't necessarily down, but the contrast is still there.

My office is based at home. I have a standing desk, which I built myself. I work at home all morning, standing up.

Things are reasonably quiet here. Besides any scheduled phone calls noisiest thing that happens in the morning is the arrival of the postman.

In the afternoon I will sometimes take my laptop and walk into Sheffield city centre. The walk is just over three miles, and passes through a park. On the walk I will catch up on podcasts.

Once in town I will go to a coffee shop, where I will write for two hours. The noise and bustle of the coffee shop contrasts to the walk and the morning of studious silence.

Contrast makes your days interesting in the same way it makes your stories interesting. The timeline provides a visual check to make sure your stories contain enough ups and downs.

Additional elements in your timeline toolkit are context (marked on the timeline with a 'C'), suspense (marked with an 'S'), and conflict (marked with an 'X').

The context of the story is the situation. Who, where, when, how, why. If you tell me a story about a mistake you once made with one of your clients, then at some point you need to tell me the context. You need to tell me who the client was, and what sort of work you were doing for them.

The most obvious place to include this context is at the beginning of the story, because that is where it fits chronologically. If you were to tell the story in order from start to finish you would start by explaining the context at the beginning.

Your story needs to contain context somewhere, and as you get to grips with this process the easiest place to include the context is at the beginning of the story. It is however perfectly legitimate to start in the thick of the action and come back to explain the context later.

> Hi Rob,
>
> We pulled up at a beautiful pink house in the Colombian countryside. I climbed off the back of the motorbike. My driver climbs off too. After a few brief 'hola's' he hands me his helmet. Hands me his jacket. Gives me the key. And asks me what time I'm going to be back...
>
> *Shit.*
>
> In 2009 I spent six weeks visiting Colombia. I spent a weekend in a town called San Augustin, in the south of the country. Nearby there are pre-Colombian burial sites you can visit. They're quite spread out, so you need transport to get between them.
>
> My travelling companion Jenny disappeared off on a horse. I view horses as animals to be admired, but not ridden. So instead, in my finest travellers Spanish,

(Full size image: https://goo.gl/xus2JJ)

Notice in this email that I start in the action, and loop back to explain the context afterwards.

If this is your first time working through the seven-step process I suggest you stick to telling the story chronologically, with the context at the beginning marked on the timeline with a 'C'. Context addresses the journalist questions of who, what, where, how and why. You don't need to address all of those questions, but the reader must understand the setting of the story.

Do not rush the timeline

If your timeline is badly planned you will only multiply problems for yourself later on. Most people spend too much time writing and not enough time planning.

The timeline will provide the blueprint for your story that will be expanded out as we follow the subsequent steps. You could think of the timeline as an uninflated balloon. In each subsequent step we will push more air into the balloon until we have a completed email.

Step 3: The 'Speedy First Draft'

The Speedy First Draft is where you take your timeline and get it down on paper as a first draft.

For most people the hardest step in the process is to get something down on paper. Most people are better at editing than writing. Once you have a first draft in place, chopping and refining it into a workable email becomes a doable endeavour. The big challenge is to get it down in the first place.

To create the Speedy First Draft, you need to focus on one timeline element at a time. At this point the only timeline elements we are looking at are context, ups and downs. If you already have suspense and conflict on your timeline you can ignore those elements for the moment.

Each timeline element is given exactly one paragraph in your Speedy First Draft, and **one paragraph only**. All you are doing at this point is explaining what is happening at that point in the story, in punchy short sentences. Elsewhere I refer to this as 'bullet point type sentences'. One way to do this is to write a series of bullet points explaining what is happening at that particular point on the timeline, and then remove all the bullets so the sentences flow from one to the next.

Take for example the following timeline:

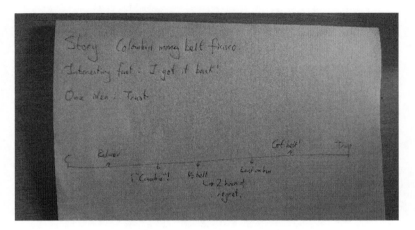

(Full size colour image: https://goo.gl/C0tpnx)

This timeline was converted into the following Speedy First Draft:

Story: Colombia bus story
One Idea: Trust

Some context – Year was 2009. On a bus between Cartagena and Santa Marta. Four-hour journey. Baking hot. I had taken off my money belt.

I had relaxed after the hectic time in Cartagena. Beautiful countryside.

In Barranquilla a guard came on. "Cambio!" All change - panic! Grabbed stuff and got off the bus.

I could still see the bus driving away, and patted my belly. No money belt. No passport. No cards. No money. My flight home was in a week.

Spoke to next bus driver. The conductor said she would make some calls. We got on. Two hours of regret.

Everyone else got off the bus, until we were the last ones on. We went to get off and were told to wait.

The conductor reappeared with my belt. Another bus company had searched that bus and got it back to me. I gave her a hug.

Link – trust.

(Full size colour image: https://goo.gl/s481u7)

I colour code the ups green and the downs red. This provides a second check for contrast, allowing you to see the ups and downs in red and green sections.

The thing to remember at this point is that the Speedy First Draft is only an interim step. It is not meant for public consumption. It is not meant to be complete. If you consider yourself to be a perfectionist you need to accept for now that your first draft will not be the polished email you're aiming for.

Perfection at this point is the enemy. Speed of production is critical.

Step 4: The Second Draft

In the second draft you will take your first draft and expand what you have written into complete sentences. We'll also start to add paragraph breaks, so a single paragraph no longer represents an entire timeline element.

I would still leave the sections colour coded for now, at least until you get to the end of this step.

(Full size colour image: https://goo.gl/PCd2Oz)

You need to remember that the second draft is still a creative process, not an editing process. At this point we are still trying to expand on the story and get more words down on paper. The point of the second draft is to blow a little more air into the balloon.

The best way to approach the second draft is to work through each sentence of your first draft, one at a time. Your focus at this point is simply to take your 'bullet point type sentences' from the first draft, and expand them into regular sentences.

We're still some way from having a complete email at this point, but in a relatively short period of time we have gone from timeline to completed draft story. Remember that the focus of both the first and second draft phases is speed, not perfection. Try to avoid slipping into editing mode. There will be plenty of time to edit the email later.

Step 5: Check for suspense or intrigue

With intrigue and suspense the idea is to worry your reader, or keep them guessing.

We all know that every story has a beginning, middle and end. What most people cannot see is that the flow from beginning, middle to end occurs throughout a story at multiple levels. It occurs at plot level, chapter level, right down to sentence level.

Even sentences have a beginning, middle and end. For example, consider the following:

```
"Rob picked up the book."
```

'Rob' is the beginning. 'Picked up' is the middle. 'The book' is the end. As you read the sentence the mental image that appears in your mind is updated. When you read the word Rob, a mental image pops up in your mind. Perhaps you have an Uncle Rob, or a friend called Rob. The mental image begins with your existing mental association with the subject.

At 'picked up', that mental image is revised. Suddenly whoever you imagined as Rob is bending down to pick something up. But what is he picking up?

'The book' then completes the mental image, and at this microscopic level provides us with our ending, or new subject. This is how the images of your imagination change as you read.

Intrigue comes from the fact that your brain is always trying to predict, or 'future-pace' what will come next. Depending on the context of the sentence, we may also know that 'Rob' was in a library, looking for a particular book. In this context, the new subject of 'the book' is entirely predictable.

If the sentence instead read:

```
"Rob picked up the alligator."
```

That would make a more intriguing sentence, because it interrupted the pattern you were expecting to appear. As the writer I would then have to justify what I have said, perhaps explaining the alligator was a small toy alligator left on the floor. You can't just pair together random words; the sentence still has to make sense.

Intrigue and suspense are different levels of the same thing. Intrigue introduces a question into your reader's mind. Suspense introduces worry. Suspense is about planting an idea and withholding the outcome of the story for a *little bit longer*.

Take for example the following email excerpt:

Subject: What to do in a robbery

Dear (name),

Have you ever been robbed, close up in person?

One September night in 2007 I was walking home about 11PM. The fastest route home passed a derelict university building under renovation.

As I walked, two boys appeared at the top of the road. Both had hoods up. One was whistling.

"Excuse me pal! Excuse me!" I stopped and turned around. "Do you know where Broomhill is?"

They continued to walk up to me. As they got closer I could see that one was smoking a spliff. Both were about my height, perhaps taller. They positioned themselves either side of me.

"Yeah, back up the road, left and right at the top," I replied.

The taller one straightened up for a moment. "Just hand your phone over," he says.

For a second we stood there watching each other. In those brief moments rational thought evaporates with a jolt of fear.

I turned and sprinted back up the road. Thirty metres. Twenty metres. I could hear the 'thump thump thump' of pounding footsteps behind me. I reached the junction with no space to turn. I ran blindly in to the road...

Do you want to know the ending to that story? Withholding the outcome of your story creates suspense, and suspense keeps people reading. To keep people reading you must keep them guessing.

I will normally identify one or two points on the timeline where I can add suspense into the story, or enhance naturally-occurring suspense. The timeline for the email above looks like this, with suspense marked as an 'S'.

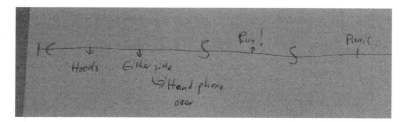

People will read long stories and long passages of text, but only when they are intrigued by the possible outcome of the story.

Suspense works on a macro and micro level. In the email above suspense is factored into the overall structure of the story, but also at sentence level. Sentences such as 'they positioned themselves either side of me' work to raise questions in your mind. Almost every sentence in the email works to build suspense in some way.

You should also consider how the pace of the email changes. Short sentences increase the pace, longer sentences slow things down. Adding suspense to your email is like holding your reader's hand and running towards the edge of a cliff. The reader cannot see what is over the edge of the cliff, and the pace is the speed at which you run towards the precipice.

There is a risk of going over-board on suspense. If every email you write tries to scare your readers the suspense loses weight after a while. Suspense is a tool to use judiciously, in just the right places.

Intrigue is the simple act of planting a question in your reader's mind and withholding the answer. Suspense is the act of planting a question, holding your reader's hand, and running with them towards the edge of the cliff.

The danger in suspense does not always have to be physical peril. It could be shame, judgement, or some kind of emotional pain. One of the tools you can use to create suspense is conflict.

Conflict

When I was small I always wondered why people watched soap operas like *EastEnders* and *Coronation Street*. To my eyes all everyone did in these programmes was fight.

Coronation Street has been running continuously since 9th December 1960. EastEnders premiered on 19th February 1985.

Both shows are older than me.

I tell people I have a twenty-year communications plan for my email list. People don't always believe me, but I'm serious. If you sign up for my email list and you find it useful I will still be writing to you every day in twenty years time. If Coronation Street can do it, so can I.

How does a show like Coronation Street keep your attention over a span of decades? They have many ups and downs in the storyline, but they also have **conflict**.

Conflict in a story can not only signify a change in direction (e.g. from 'up' to 'down'), it also means that some sort of character development is happening.

Character development is what we really want from a story. Next time you watch a great film, the question to ask isn't 'what happened?' The question to ask is 'who changed?' Which characters by the end of the story have grown up, overcome their ego, or otherwise rounded off some sort of personality flaw?

Take *The Jungle Book* again as an example. *The Jungle Book* is a growing-up story, with Mowgli as the lead character. There is a false ending partway through the film when Baloo reluctantly marches Mowgli to the man-village. On discovering their destination, Mowgli dashes off into the under-growth. In terms of character development he wasn't ready to go to the man-village. The growing-up theme behind the story was not yet complete.

Only after Mowgli has escaped Kaa's coils and the clutches of Shere Khan does he join the man-village, and the film ends. The story can only end once the personal transformation of the lead character is complete, and personal change comes about through conflict. Without conflict a story is dull.

Conflict works in your emails just as it works in the movies. Most companies avoid using conflict, worrying that by including conflict they will somehow appear negative. You cannot sugar-coat the stories you produce and expect people to engage emotionally with them.

We engage with conflict because we recognise it as a part of day-to-day life. Conflict also exposes the main character's flaws. We see that the main character is not perfect. This vulnerability allows us to connect with him or her, because we recognise the flaws in our own lives.

Conflict in a story involves struggle. We enjoy a good story because we enjoy watching the hero wrestle with the dark characters of the story. The 'dark character' may not be a person; it may be an addiction or vice.

The real purpose of conflict is as a catalyst for personal change. Real personal change does not happen in good times. Real personal change happens in bad times with the associated conflict. People don't change unless their immediate situation is untenable.

There are three types of conflict you can use in your emails: physical, emotional and reflective.

Physical Conflict

I have only ever been in one proper fight, and it was with a friend called Tony.

We were in year six, which would have made us ten or eleven. One bright spring day at lunch I went to the boys room and found Tony standing at a urinal. Spotting the opportunity for a cheap laugh, I gave him a shove forward.

Tony turned round and exploded. "That's it!" he yelled. "We're having a FIGHT after school".

There is something viral about the word 'fight' in a school environment. It seems to travel on the wind all of its own accord.

That afternoon random strangers came up to me to offer advice, and sparring practice.

In the two hours between lunch and the end of school Tony and I shared the same classes. The classes had what you might call 'an atmosphere'. I would occasionally look at Tony. He would refuse to look at me. You could hear the word *fight* travelling around on the breeze, etched in to people's faces.

At half past three the end-of-school bell rang – ding ding ding! Fight-time. We headed around to the back of the school, followed closely by thirty excited onlookers.

I think at this point I would have backed down, but fight hysteria has a self-sustaining snowball effect. "Fight fight fight FIGHT," chanted the crowd. Squaring up to Tony I raised my fists. Tony did the same.

"COME 'ED! Hit him!" someone shouted from the outside.

Suddenly Tony burst forward. This was it. We were actually going to fight.

The fight itself didn't last more than a minute or two. We threw a few punches. I took a few hits – the sort that make blood race to your head. A teacher heard the commotion and came out to stop the fight.

The next day once the hysteria had died I apologised to Tony when we were alone. He accepted my apology. We now joke about it occasionally when I threaten to push him into the loo.

I remember this story with great clarity because the lesson was crystal clear. Cheap laughs at someone else's expense aren't funny. And take responsibility for your screw-ups.

It was an event that caused a small revision in my personality. Had the fight not happened I do not believe the revision would have happened. I doubt I would even remember the incident.

Physical conflict in your stories always introduces a degree of suspense. If you were to map the story above on a timeline it would look something like this:

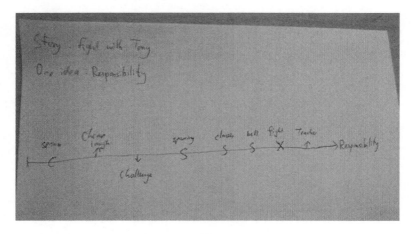

(Full size image: https://goo.gl/GkhpxS)

The conflict is marked with an 'X'. Notice how the suspense builds up before the fight, as marked by the three 'S's'.

Emotional Conflict

A few years ago I received a new AdWords lead for my AdWords management service. George* had been reading my emails for a few months, and decided one day to get in touch.

George's company was using AdWords to generate leads for an offline sales process. The company was spending £25,000 a month on AdWords (about $35,000). Which for me was a large account.

George mentioned on the phone they had 'been through' quite a few AdWords agencies. But he'd like to 'see what I could do'.

On the eve of the project George sent me an email in badly-formatted English. 'I'd like a daily report please Rob', the email said. 'The report should show yesterday's spend by campaign, click through rate, conversions and cost per conversion.'

I've never sent daily reports to clients because daily fluctuations can be misleading. Weekly numbers are more meaningful. And monthly numbers never lie.

I've also since learnt that clients who demand a daily report are usually spending more than their resources will allow. Clients who panic about a daily drop in conversions are usually flying a little close to the sun.

I always knew if the conversions were down for the day, because at 3PM I would get an email. 'URGENT Leads down Rob. Please action ASAP.'

Things like this make me rage. Please action what? I'm not a magician. Most of the time I would ignore it and rely on a natural upturn in leads the following day.

I've also since learnt that clients who routinely send emails with URGENT in the subject line, signed off with 'ASAP' are not great clients to work with. It's a small clue that they see you as a vendor to be used, not an expert to be consulted.

Not long after the project had started I made a bunch of changes to the website, and George blew his lid. "We make changes on a month by month basis," he informed me. "That way we compare apples to apples."

Apples to apples – yeah right. You can't have it all ways up. You can't scream and shout about your AdWords results, but also refuse to make any changes to the website.

The project fizzled out after a few months. I was glad, too. The hassle wasn't worth the management fee they paid me. Or so I thought.

One year later George got back in touch. His last business had tanked, and now he had a new business in another highly competitive market.

George asked if I would consider managing the account again, since I had 'done such a good job last time'. I wavered for a moment. The warning signs were all there. I knew George was a well-meaning but troublesome client. But I also needed the revenue.

So we went again. This time George wasn't my main point of contact; he had a marketing manager, Jane*. Jane was nice enough, but clearly under huge pressure to perform. Once again I failed to set the boundaries on when I could and could not be contacted.

At 9.50 every morning my phone would go (Jane started work at 10). Despite my repeated warnings about daily statistics she would want to discuss yesterday's numbers, and know 'what I was doing for them today'.

"Nothing," was the response I should have given. "You're paying me for results, not graft, sweat and labour."

I didn't have the gall to say that at the time.

A few weeks later I went to Italy for a week. I tried to reassure Jane that her AdWords results were unlikely to tank for a few days without my daily hand-holding. I had no phone signal in Italy, and no computer.

Two days in to our holiday I logged on to Wi-Fi in my hotel, and my phone buzzed to life. WhatsApp. It was Jane. "URGENT: NO conversions yesterday. George won't stand for it. Please look at this ASAP."

Really Jane? You're going to harass me on holiday... by *WhatsApp*?

After three months of emotional conflict our second project came to an end. George finally discovered that I had been ruining his monthly 'apples to apples' comparison by sending traffic to pages other than the homepage.

Emotional conflict is our second type of conflict. Emotional conflict still occurs between you and another individual or entity, the only difference is nobody gets physically bruised.

That isn't to say it doesn't hurt. Emotional conflict can hurt just as much as physical conflict. It can keep you awake at night. It can make you dread going to work.

The point in using emotional conflict in your stories is to:

- Expose your mistakes and show you are human. Everybody can relate to emotional conflict.

- Add a degree of drama. The drama stakes are not as high as physical conflict. But your readers should be wondering what your nightmare opponent is going to do next.

- Illustrate learning. The project with George was ultimately my fault. I saw the warning signs. I failed to set boundaries. I accepted the project. TWICE!

The final type of conflict comes back to haunt you later on...

*Name changed for privacy.

Reflective Conflict

Reflective conflict is the mind-chatter that goes on in your head. Rather than fight with another person you end up fighting with yourself. Reflective conflict is about the universal human notion of choice and dilemma. Reflective conflict is the most subtle form of conflict.

Nikki, one of my copywriting students, recently sent me the following email excerpt to review:

> Pete, my husband of 29 years walked into the home office where I was working. He cleared his throat.
>
> "Hey Nik, I've just spoken with a TV producer who wants us to appear on a documentary about infidelity. Is that something you would be interested in?'
>
> He eyed me curiously, trying to gauge my reaction.
>
> Would I be horrified by the prospect of this? After all, just four short years ago I would rather have poked red hot needles in my eyes than let anyone know my hubby had cheated on me. I certainly would not have contemplated broadcasting it on national TV.
>
> I paused and considered the request for a moment. Then I…

Reflective conflict is unlikely to ever be a story in its own right, more often it will be a paragraph or two within a story.

There are two reasons to use reflective conflict in your writing.

The first is that reflective conflict makes you vulnerable. In effect you are offering the reader a peek into the inner secrets of your head. This vulnerability is what creates real emotional connection. You can't emotionally connect with somebody who has their guard up all the time.

The second reason is to add intrigue. Nikki could have cut out the reflective paragraph beginning 'Would I be horrified', but the writing would be less intriguing. Reflective conflict delays giving your reader the answer to the question you have posed. Intrigue, suspense and conflict are all related.

The reflective conflict paragraph has been set up by a much shorter intriguing sentence; 'He eyed me curiously, trying to gauge my reaction.'

Reflective conflict paragraphs tend to be longer than average. You are trying to work things out in your head, and this takes more space on the page. The correct way to lead in to a reflective paragraph is to deliver a short sentence that underlines the question in the reader's mind.

We have covered a lot in the last few pages. Step five in our seven steps has looked at suspense and intrigue as tools to keep people reading your stories. We've looked at three types of conflict that can create intrigue and suspense in a story.

Once you have checked for suspense and conflict you can move on to the reconnect.

Step 6: The reconnect

The reconnect is the point at which your story ends and your content begins. In the reconnect you write two specific sentences that end your story and begin your content on your one idea.

Story: Colombia bus story
One Idea: Trust

The year was 2009. I was travelling on a bus between Cartagena and Santa Marta, with my travelling companions Jenny and Alan.

I had relaxed on the bus after a hectic three days in Cartagena. As we passed beautiful Colombian countryside I unclipped my money belt to make myself more comfortable.

Halfway to Santa Marta a guard came on. "Cambio! Cambio!" he shouted. All change! For half a second I panicked, grabbed my stuff and got off the bus.

As the bus drove away I tentatively patted my stomach where my money belt would normally sit. It was missing.

My stomach sank. No money belt meant no passport. No credit cards. No money. My flight home to London was in a week.

In my finest traveller's Spanish I frantically explained to the next bus conductor what had happened. Looking grave she told us to get on, and promised she would make some calls. We glanced at each other and got on the bus.

Around us locals were chatting. Some were talking about football, others wanted to talk to us about England. All I could think was every passing second meant travelling further away from my passport.

After two hours we arrived in Santa Marta, and one by one everyone else departed. Eventually we were the only ones on the bus. The conductor disappeared, and the driver switched off the engine.

Just as we were about to leave the conductor reappeared, clutching my belt. She told us that another bus company had searched that bus and got it back to me. I gave her a hug. A few dollars were missing, but my passport and credit cards were still there.

Despite all the horror stories you hear of tourists being robbed in South America, I thought this was a great example of trust.

In my experience trust is a major reason why people choose Infusionsoft as their email marketing platform. Your prospects have to know like and trust you before they will buy, so you need a system that enables you to build up that trust over a longer period of time.

There are four reasons why you should book a demo with me to discuss Infusionsoft. First...

(Full size colour image: https://goo.gl/HGZCe5)

The two reconnect sentences have been highlighted red. The one idea that links story to content in this case is trust. Note in the reconnect that 'trust' has been mentioned at the *end* of the story sentence and the *beginning* of the content sentence.

Once you understand the full seven-step process you will start to select the one idea for your story with half an eye on the reconnect. In theory you could connect any story with any content using any reconnect, but in practice it will often feel forced. Selecting a one idea that feels related to the content will make your email feel less patched up.

The power of the reconnect is you no longer have to perfectly match stories and content. You can pair up loosely related stories and content, and link them seamlessly using the reconnect.

The story part of your email is like taking your reader on a walk through the park.

Your Story = A Walk In The PARK

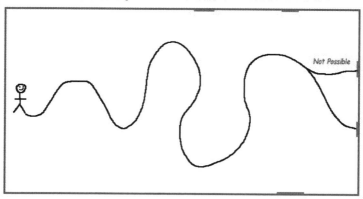

Not Possible

The story can contain ups, downs and conflict. The route to the park exit is never linear, or else the story would be meaningless. At the end of the story you have a choice of gates, where each gate represents a possible reconnect. You can only leave the story and move on to the content through **one** of the gates.

Once you have completed the reconnect you are ready to add your content. I am going to say remarkably little about content in this book, because your content is probably already good. Most people struggle with the story portion of the email, but find that the content part comes naturally. The content is simply the email content you would write if you included no story whatsoever.

Step 7: Editing

Most people are better editors than they are writers. I think I'm a better writer, but I also love to edit. Perhaps because as a writer, I love nothing more than to read my own beautiful writing.

The challenge when you are starting out is to completely separate the writing and editing processes, and leave sufficient time in between to reflect on the writing.

I will often write out an email, and decide in the heat of the moment that Shakespeare himself couldn't have written better prose. I'll then put it aside and sleep on it overnight. The next day I'll read it back, and wonder exactly what I was thinking.

No matter how good you get at this your writing **always** suffers when writing and editing happen too close together.

Steps 1-6 are expansive steps, where we are expanding the body of our email and blowing out the balloon a little more. Editing is a reduction step, meaning we are going to chop parts of your writing away. Because of this distinction, writing and editing use your brain in a completely different way. If you try to edit as you go, you snap your brain out of a creative process every time you move into 'editing mode'. It is far more efficient to only make the transition once.

When it comes to email production, efficiency is everything. It is no good you following this process if it takes you seven days to produce an email. You need to be producing emails in hours, not days. Maybe even in under an hour, before anyone else even arrives at work.

I talk at greater length about editing in my course, Nurture Email Mastery, but I will leave you here with my editing rules of thumb. These rules are the 80/20 of editing. Principles that when applied will give you 80% of the editing result in 20% of the time.

Rule #1: Humble beginnings

Most of my emails start with a short paragraph, maybe just a simple short sentence. When a reader encounters your first sentence they will still be debating whether to go ahead and read the full email. You could consider your reader to be like a fish, nibbling at your bait.

If your first paragraph is four lines long there is a good chance you will scare away your reader.

Rule #2: One paragraph = one idea

Each paragraph should only cover one idea. As soon as you find yourself moving on to a new idea you normally need a paragraph break. When you are writing an email you need to be careful with paragraph length because it is so easy to lose the reader.

Most of the paragraphs in my emails contain two or three sentences. It is the variation in sentence length that causes the different paragraph sizes.

Rule #3: Simple sentences

The (1) easiest (2) sentence (3) to (4) read (5) contains (6) eight (7) words (8). The average sentence length is 16 words. Any sentence above 32 words is entering the snooze-zone.

The length of your sentences will vary throughout your email, but on the whole you want to average closer to eight than thirty.

The variation in length is important. If you were to take the advice in this section at face value and only ever write sentences of eight words, you would end up with a children's book.

When people read your emails they actually read with a voice in their head. The voice has a rhythm, and that rhythm comes from varied sentence length.

Variation aside, if you can convey the same message in a shorter sentence without losing any of the emotional impact, then do so. Editing is all about refining your ideas, eliminating rough edges, and making sure the emotion you are trying to convey comes across.

Rule #4: Take your time

Most writers are obsessed with email length. People **will** read longer emails if the story is good and the content interesting.

You want your emails to be as efficient as possible. But you also want your emails to be empowering, deeply meaningful and insightful.

'Taking your time' does not mean that you take your time to complete the writing itself. Most of my writing is produced quickly, usually under the looming threat of a deadline. The trick is to take your time illustrating and delivering your point.

The emails you send should never *look like* they were prepared in a rush, even if that was the case. The emails you send should look like they were leisurely drafted from your Mediterranean villa while you perused the morning papers over coffee.

Taking your time can also mean adding a little white space. White space in your emails comes from paragraph breaks. You can introduce more white space by adding a short paragraph.

A paragraph like this.

Notice the white space? The white space comes from a contrast between the different lengths of the paragraphs, which is why variation is so important in both sentence and paragraph length.

Rule #5: Look out for empty words

Watch out for 'enhancing' words like *very, fantastic, great, superb* and so on. When these words are used the writer is normally trying to enhance the significance of what follows. The problem with using these words is it sounds like you are trying too hard to draw my attention to the things you think are important.

Your readers will decide what is important all by themselves. There is no need to enhance the importance of something with empty words that add no meaning to the sentence. If you use the word 'very' for example, it should be to describe close proximity, not that something was exceptionally good.

Another word that can be removed in 50% of instances is the word 'that':

All I could think was that every passing second meant travelling further away from my passport.

All I could think was every passing second meant travelling further away from my passport.

Rule #6: Use better verbs

English language was never my strongest subject at school. Just in case it wasn't your favourite subject either, verbs are *doing* words. Kick, scrub, swipe, write, scrawl, scoop.

Often you can improve an email by simply auditing the verbs:

Before anyone else arrived at the office this morning I wrote out an email...

Before anyone else arrived at the office this morning I scrawled out an email...

Notice the difference? Better verbs help to bring your reader into the story.

Rule #7: Write in active, not passive voice

Active sentences describe cause before effect. John kicked the ball. I wrote the email.

Passive sentences describe the effect before the cause. The ball was kicked by John. The email was written by you.

Passive sentences are a feature of academic writing because a passive sentence distances the author from proceedings, and makes things feel more objective. When you write a marketing email the **last** thing you want to be is objective. You want instead to persuade, and persuasion requires active sentences.

A clue you are slipping into passive voice can be seen when you include lots of words ending in 'ing'. John was kick**ing** the ball, when...

Suddenly you're objectively describing what John was doing, not telling me that John kicked the ball, which was the point of the sentence.

I actually slip into passive voice quite a lot. It's terribly easy, which is why writing and editing are completely different skills.

The best writers are rarely excellent editors (although a degree of competency can help). And the best editors are rarely excellent writers. Still, keep an eye out for passive voice as you edit your work.

When to stop editing

The problem with editing is it never ends. You could edit an email for days making minor tweaks, changes and improvements.

Achieving perfection is not the objective of editing. An email you send today is always more effective than one that goes tomorrow. The editing process suffers from what economists call diminishing returns. You'll see big improvements in the initial stages of editing, but as time goes on the changes turn into minor tweaks.

At this point you need to stop editing and send the email.

Part 2 Summary

Part 2 of the book has been about *getting going*. We've looked at why opening your emails with a story can be an effective lead, and we've broken down the complicated process of story creation into a series of steps.

In Part 3, we'll take your stories to the next level and make them truly evergreen.

Part 3: Applying the plot archetypes to your stories

You may remember from Part 1 that the presence of a 'plot archetype' was an ingredient of a persuasive, evergreen story. In this final part of the book, we look at each plot archetype in more detail, and look at how they can be used in your marketing.

This part of the book began as an experiment. At the start of 2016, I emailed my list and told them I would send them one archetypal story per day, for a week. I wanted to discover whether the plot archetypes Christopher Booker had identified in his book *The Seven Basic Plots* could be used for practical 'real life' business purposes.

The results were promising, but a little mixed. Some of the plots applied better to my own business than others. I could see huge potential in the 'overcoming the monster' plot, but I struggled to create a business story out of 'the quest'. I could think of some clients where the quest would be highly appropriate. But because I rarely travel anywhere, my number of potential 'quest' stories felt more limited.

As we go through this section, some of the plots will be more usable to you than others, depending on the nature of your business. I suggest you read the following section through to build a complete understanding of the seven plots, but then select one or two to implement in your marketing. Your origin story is often a good place to employ an archetypal plot. I would tell your origin story as an introduction sequence, when people first sign up for your emails.

You might remember from Part 1 that every archetypal story has five distinct phases.

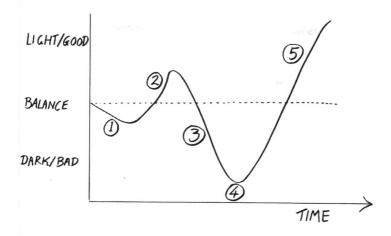

As we work through each plot, I've provided guidance on things you might include in each section. Let's look at each plot in more detail.

1. Overcoming the Monster

Overcoming the monster is the most important and best known story archetype. Examples include *The Epic of Gilgamesh, Jaws, Star Wars, The Hobbit, Jurassic Park*. The overcoming the monster plot is always centred around a hero who must undergo various trials, tribulations and setbacks before finally overcoming a dark enemy.

I believe the overcoming the monster plot is effective because it taps into a human impulse I call the 'big cat template'.

Every year in Britain, roughly 2000 sightings of big cats are reported to the police. People mostly report pumas or panthers, or simply describe a 'beast'.

Despite the 'sightings', we can categorically say there are no big cats left in Britain in the 21st Century. Cats like pumas and panthers are actually easy to find. Big cats leave conspicuous evidence of their presence, including territories, dens, spraying points and scratching posts. None of that evidence can be seen anywhere in Britain today.

So why is it that so many people report seeing these big cats?

The threat of attack from predators like big cats only receded from human life in the Western world about 20,000 years ago. In evolutionary terms, you still have a 'big cat programme' running in your brain. If your brain sees something that looks *anything like* a big cat, it activates the big cat programme and tells you to run.

Monsters still haunt our subconscious brain, even though the real-life threat from those monsters has now receded. Which means that when an 'overcoming the monster' plot comes along, we pay attention.

Overcoming the monster is a simple plot because there is a clear and obvious distinction between good and bad forces in the story. The dark force in the story is entirely contained within the monster, while the hero or heroine is presented with light or innocent qualities. We are in no doubt as to who is the monster and who is the hero.

In literature, the monster is always 'deadly', threatening the hero and the world at large with destruction. Often the monster will have some sort of treasure or 'prize' in its clutches, which it will jealously guard.

The five stages of the 'overcoming the monster' plot are as follows:

1. Anticipation / call

We are introduced to both the hero and the monster. The monster is usually described as ruthless, menacing, poisonous, cunning, treacherous, slippery, vile. The monster may be described as being strange, dark or deformed.

In the anticipation stage the monster makes its dark power and cruel intentions known, perhaps annihilating a friend or family member of the hero. In *Star Wars*, the planet Alderaan is blown up by the newly constructed 'death star'.

2. Dream stage

Our hero makes good progress against the monster. Our hero may achieve an initial or moral victory. Things for a while go well.

3. Frustration stage

The full power of the monster finally comes out of the shadows, and into full view. The Tyrannosaurus Rex escapes from its enclosure in *Jurassic Park*. Darth Vader tricks and overpowers Luke Skywalker in *The Empire Strikes Back*.

4. Climax / final ordeal

In a 'final ordeal', the monster is finally confronted by our hero. For a while, it looks with all certainty like the monster will win. The cunning Velociraptors slowly corner the heroes of *Jurassic Park*. The Emperor looks poised to destroy Luke Skywalker in *Return of the Jedi*.

5. Miraculous escape and reward

The monster will usually overlook something in its single-minded quest for gratification, which is the source of its eventual downfall.

The Velociraptors somehow fail to spot the approaching T-Rex. The shark in *Jaws* is finally outwitted by an exploding scuba tank. Our hero makes a miraculous escape from the (sometimes literal) jaws of certain death, and claims his or her reward.

How to translate this into a business story

Overcoming the monster is perhaps the most useful plot archetype from a business perspective. Story examples could include:

- A nightmare boss
- A nightmare employee
- A nightmare customer
- A business partner who worked against your interests
- A nightmare supplier
- A colleague who stole your promotion
- A competitor whose sole all-consuming desire seemed to be putting you out of business

Think about all of the times somebody has tried to screw you over at work, and you have a potential 'overcoming the monster' story.

The monster in the story has to be personally out to get you. The monster's goal in the story is your personal downfall or destruction, often for little more purpose than to fuel their own ego.

The monster is always egocentric. Despite its cunning, its awareness of the world around it is in some way limited. The distortion of ego means it cannot see things for what they really are. It truly believes in its own lies.

No character in a business story will ever be 100% monster in real life, but that isn't to say you cannot present them as 100% monster in your story. For an overcoming the monster story to be effective, the monster should not be given any positive, empathetic or redeeming qualities.

Overcoming the Monster Example

Subject: Have you ever kept a diary... about your boss?

Hi ~Contact.FirstName~,

Imran burst up out of his seat, furious.

"I am your manager! You do as I say!" he quivered at me in rage.

I got up out of my chair, and stormed out of the room. I wouldn't be spoken to like that. This was war.

—

In 2007 I took a placement-year job with a small software company near London.

During the recruitment process I had been introduced to the marketing manager JB. JB explained how the marketing team put significant effort into tracking where every enquiry came from. This, as you can imagine, was music to my young direct marketing ears.

By the time I started work, JB had ominously moved on to another department. We were told not to worry; a new marketing manager was starting in two weeks.

Two weeks later a dented Toyota Corolla pulled up at the office and Imran* stepped out. He introduced himself with a limp handshake, and we walked around the office.

"Where have you come from, Imran?" I asked.

"Oh, from Microsoft," he replied vaguely.

Getting specifics from Imran was like nailing jelly to the wall. Much later on I got hold of a copy of his cliché-laden CV and discovered the company had never even checked his references.

My marketing colleague at the time was PK, another placement student.

"I don't like him man, he gives me a bad feeling," complained PK that night.

"It'll be okay," I reassured. "It's only day one..."

For a few weeks, things were okay. Imran spent the first week presenting his devious plans to top management. PK and I were left mostly alone, to get on with the real work of implementing the marketing plan.

We quickly realised that the only work Imran was capable of accomplishing was nervously watching the shared email inbox where enquiries would arrive. Whenever he was nervous or didn't understand something, which was all the time, he would shake his legs.

One morning I was drafting an email to go to our customer list, when Imran suddenly spun around on his chair.

"Rob," he began, "how many leads do we have?"

"I don't know Imran," I replied without turning round. "Have a look yourself." I could feel his beady eyes staring into the back of my head.

Later that week I called one of our print designers. We had a few designers we worked with who knew us well. Sometimes we would press them for a better price, sometimes not.

Imran wasn't interested in any of this.

"We get three quotes, three quotes every time!" he yelled at me across the room. "And we choose the cheapest!"

I had a proposal from our designer printer I wanted to move ahead with, and told the designer as much, ignoring Imran's whisperings from behind me. He exploded in rage, screaming "I am your manager! You do as I say!"

Shortly afterwards, Imran asked me to BCC him in to every email I sent. (I did not). He also insisted that every marketing email we sent out went via him for 'proofreading'.

I would draft a perfectly good email (or 'eshot', as he called it). Imran would read it for a while, shaking his legs in confusion. Eventually he would pull out a red pen and delete random essential passages.

As a writer, nothing is more infuriating.

Both Imran and I reported each other's behaviour to senior management. He obviously wanted to work with someone more 'pliable'. And I wasn't willing to be yelled at by someone I viewed as an incompetent control freak. I was called into SD's office. SD was Imran's boss.

"If what you're saying is true," SD started, "then this is a serious disciplinary issue. But we need specific evidence."

After that I started to keep an 'Imran diary'. Imran decided it was amusing to forward emails to me from the spam folder about penis extension. That went in the diary. I kept a record of how often he was late to work. I even kept a loose record of how much time he spent shaking his legs in perplexity at the leads inbox. Every few weeks I would send an update to SD, from my personal email so Imran couldn't see what I was up to.

Imran won the battle about my emails. Every email I sent would be automatically CC'd to Imran. Which meant that every time I sent an email his laptop would 'ding'! He'd stop shaking his legs for a few seconds while he snooped on what I had sent.

Six months into the job, I'd had enough. Even at 21, I believed that life was too short to spend my time working with cretins. I liked the company and I liked the people, but I couldn't work any longer with Imran. Somewhat annoyingly, his monthly marketing numbers had been good.

I shared a whisky with PK one evening, and drafted my letter of resignation. The letter was short and to the point, but it stated my reasons clearly. In my slightly intoxicated state I had planned to go in the next morning and staple it to Imran's face.

The sun rose the following morning on a crisp, sunny winters day. I walked through the door at work with butterflies in my stomach. Imran, of course, was late. As soon as he arrived, SD approached. "Imran, I'd like a word please," he said in a clear voice. By now my notice letter was practically burning a hole in my pocket.

SD and Imran disappeared into a meeting room. From inside, I could hear animated voices. After a full hour, Imran emerged from the meeting room. He picked up his bag, shot me a death-stare, and stormed quickly out of the office.

SD later told me that Imran had been fabricating his numbers. In the meeting Imran had first tried to pin the blame on me, and then argued they should fire the previous marketing manager JB, instead.

A month later he also tried to sue the company for commissions owed from leads generated. He thought he was on a £100 per lead commission, which looking back explains his daily paranoia about the leads count.

PK and I were left in charge of the marketing for the rest of the year. My resignation letter stayed firmly in my pocket.

(Link to content)

(Email signature)

*Name changed for privacy.

Notes

Like many of the story archetypes, Overcoming the Monster can be more effective when told over a slightly longer format. In an email sequence, you might want to consider splitting the story over two or three emails, dwelling particularly on the frustration stage (stage 3).

I wanted to illustrate here that it *is* possible to tell a full overcoming the monster plot in a single email. Yes, the story is longer than your average email. Length however is not a problem if the email keeps your attention.

The stages in the email look like this.

Stages Walkthrough

Stage 1: Anticipation / call
Stage 2: Dream stage
Stage 3: Frustration stage
Stage 4: Climax / final ordeal
Stage 5: Miraculous escape and reward

Subject: Have you ever kept a diary… about your boss?

Hi ~Contact.FirstName~,

(Start of Stage 3)

Imran burst up out of his seat, furious.

"I am your manager! You do as I say!" he quivered at me in rage.

I got up out of my chair, and stormed out of the room. I wouldn't be spoken to like that. This was war.

(End of Stage 3)

I've started in the middle of the action here, in the frustration phase. Because this is a relatively long story, I want to draw you into the action early on.

—

(Start of Stage 1)

In 2007 I took a placement-year job with a small software company near London.

During the recruitment process I had been introduced to the marketing manager JB. JB explained how the marketing team put significant effort into tracking where every enquiry came from. This, as you can imagine, was music to my young direct marketing ears.

By the time I started work, JB had ominously moved on to another department. We were told not to worry; a new marketing manager was starting in two weeks.

Two weeks later a dented Toyota Corolla pulled up at the office and Imran* stepped out. He introduced himself with a limp handshake, and we walked around the office.

"Where have you come from, Imran?" I asked.

"Oh, from Microsoft," he replied vaguely.

Getting specifics from Imran was like nailing jelly to the wall. Much later on I got hold of a copy of his cliché-laden CV and discovered the company had never even checked his references. My marketing colleague at the time was PK, another placement student.

"I don't like him man, he gives me a bad feeling," complained PK that night.

"It'll be okay," I reassured. "It's only day one..."

(End of Stage 1)

The anticipation phase serves to tee up the rest of the story. This may come across as 'mean' to some readers, but I've deliberately dwelt on Imran's dented car and limp handshake. The handshake is also a forewarning of what is to come.

I can't stress enough how important this is. **Do not give your monster any redeeming features.**

(Start of Stage 2)

For a few weeks, things were okay. Imran spent the first week presenting his devious plans to top management. PK and I were left mostly alone, to get on with the real work of implementing the marketing plan.

(End of Stage 2)

I've kept the 'dream' stage to a short paragraph in this example. In general the dream stage should usually be shorter than the frustration stage, although this is at your discretion.

(Start of Stage 3)

We quickly realised that the only work Imran was capable of accomplishing was nervously watching the shared email inbox where enquiries would arrive. Whenever he was nervous or didn't understand something, which was all the time, he would shake his legs.

One morning I was drafting an email to go to our customer list, when Imran suddenly spun around on his chair.

"Rob," he began, "how many leads do we have?"

"I don't know Imran," I replied without turning round. "Have a look yourself." I could feel his beady eyes staring into the back of my head.

Later that week I called one of our print designers. We had a few designers we worked with who knew us well. Sometimes we would press them for a better price, sometimes not.

Imran wasn't interested in any of this.

"We get three quotes, three quotes every time!" he yelled at me across the room. "And we choose the cheapest!"

I had a proposal from our designer printer I wanted to move ahead with, and told the designer as much, ignoring Imran's whisperings from behind me. He exploded in rage, screaming "I am your manager! You do as I say!"

Shortly afterwards, Imran asked me to BCC him in to every email I sent. (I did not). He also insisted that every marketing email we sent out went via him for 'proofreading'.

I would draft a perfectly good email (or 'eshot', as he called it). Imran would read it for a while, shaking his legs in confusion. Eventually he would pull out a red pen and delete random essential passages.

As a writer, nothing is more infuriating.

Both Imran and I reported each other's behaviour to senior management. He obviously wanted to work with someone more 'pliable'. And I wasn't willing to be yelled at by someone I viewed as an incompetent control freak. I was called into SD's office. SD was Imran's boss.

"If what you're saying is true," SD started, "then this is a serious disciplinary issue. But we need specific evidence."

After that I started to keep an 'Imran diary'. Imran decided it was amusing to forward emails to me from the spam folder about penis extension. That went in the diary. I kept a record of how often he was late to work. I even kept a loose record of how much time he spent shaking his legs in perplexity at the leads inbox. Every few weeks I would send an update to SD, from my personal email so Imran couldn't see what I was up to.

Imran won the battle about my emails. Every email I sent would be automatically CC'd to Imran. Which meant that every time I sent an email his laptop would 'ding'! He'd stop shaking his legs for a few seconds while he snooped on what I had sent.

(End of Stage 3)

I've focused in the frustration stage on Imran's leg-shaking. Again, I'm sorry if this comes across as mean, but it is essential to make the monster look like the monster, with damaged or undesirable qualities. I've also described his 'beady eyes', to give him a more reptilian image.

(Start of Stage 4)

Six months into the job, I'd had enough. Even at 21, I believed that life was too short to spend my time working with cretins. I liked the company and I liked the people, but I couldn't work any longer with Imran. Somewhat annoyingly, his monthly marketing numbers had been good.

I shared a whisky with PK one evening, and drafted my letter of resignation. The letter was short and to the point, but it stated my reasons clearly. In my slightly intoxicated state I had planned to go in the next morning and staple it to Imran's face.

The sun rose the following morning on a crisp, sunny winters day. I walked through the door at work with butterflies in my stomach. Imran, of course, was late. As soon as he arrived, SD approached. "Imran, I'd like a word please," he said in a clear voice. By now my notice letter was practically burning a hole in my pocket.

SD and Imran disappeared into a meeting room. From inside, I could hear animated voices. After a full hour, Imran emerged from the meeting room. He picked up his bag, shot me a death-stare, and stormed quickly out of the office.

(End of Stage 4)

At the climax of the story you must be on the brink of defeat. It must seem like the monster will win. Then at the last second, you have a miraculous redemption.

(Start of Stage 5)

SD later told me that Imran had been fabricating his numbers. In the meeting Imran had first tried to pin the blame on me, and then argued they should fire the previous marketing manager JB, instead.

A month later he also tried to sue the company for commissions owed from leads generated. He thought he was on a £100 per lead commission, which looking back explains his daily paranoia about the leads count.

PK and I were left in charge of the marketing for the rest of the year. My resignation letter stayed firmly in my pocket.

(End of Stage 5)

—

The story must have a resolution, and you should be rewarded for defeating the monster.

2. Rags to Riches

Rags to riches stories include *Aladdin*, *Jane Eyre*, *Great Expectations* and *The Ugly Duckling*. The rags to riches plot is essentially a growing up story, and it has wide-ranging use in business.

Unfortunately, when most marketers use this plot they skip straight to the 'bragging about their riches' part, which is not the point of the story whatsoever.

The point is to dwell on the struggles you had to overcome, the insurmountable challenges you faced, and your conflicts with various dark characters who tried to hold you back.

Rags to riches is not an excuse to brag. It is an excuse to tell people about your journey towards success.

The stages in the rags to riches plot are:

1. Initial wretchedness and 'call'

In literature, a rags to riches story always introduces us to the main character in childhood, or adolescence. The first part of the story will always emphasise how wretched or seemingly inferior our hero is. Often they will be persecuted or bullied by one or more 'dark characters' in these early stages. Aladdin is persecuted by the palace guards. Jane Eyre is bullied and rejected by her cousins. In the opening chapters of *Great Expectations*, Pip is accosted by an escaped convict.

2. Out into the world, initial success

Our young hero will step out into the world and experience some initial success. Aladdin appears to win the heart of Princess Jasmine, with his genie-inspired act as Prince Ali. Jane Eyre appears to find happiness with Mr Rochester. In *Great Expectations*, Pip is bound as an apprentice blacksmith, and discovers he has 'great expectations' from an anonymous benefactor. Everything seems to be rolling towards a happy ending.

3. The central crisis

The 'dark force' in the story reappears with a vengeance, forcing the hero into the 'central crisis'. The central crisis is usually an issue of identity. The initial success our hero experienced in stage two may have come through the hero 'putting on an act', rather than acting as their real self. Dark characters re-emerge in the story.

Aladdin is arrested by the palace guards, and vanquished by Jafar. Jane Eyre flees into the clutches of St. John Rivers.

4. Independence and final ordeal

At the climax of the story, our hero will finally overcome the forces of darkness by standing unsupported on their own two feet. Aladdin finally defeats Jafar without the help of the Genie. Most importantly, final independence is achieved by acting as their true self.

In a rags to riches plot, dark characters always represent a flaw in the hero's character that must be overcome for the objective of the story to be achieved. Jafar represents the greed and selfishness that Aladdin must overcome, if he is to win the heart of princess Jasmine. Once he achieves this, the Jafar disappears from the story.

5. Completion and fulfilment

The hero finally reveals qualities which have been in him, at least potentially, the entire time. Jane Eyre displays the strength of inner resolve that had been hinted at throughout the entire story, and rejects St. John Rivers for the blind and deformed Mr. Rochford. The ugly duckling has now transformed into a beautiful swan.

How to translate this into a business story

Most companies mess up the rags to riches plot by jumping straight from stage one to stage five. The point of the rags to riches plot is not to boast about how rich you are, or about how many rags you wore starting out. The point of the plot is to illustrate the challenging personal transformation you had to go through in between the stages, to arrive at your current situation.

We all intuitively know that real success is rarely linear. Most of us have one or more failure cycles, or central crisis, before finding our groove.

A rags to riches story in your marketing could be about:

- Your personal story
- Your company
- Your founder

Rags to Riches Example

Subject: "Can you get me to the top of Google?"

Hi ~Contact.FirstName~,

In summer 2012 I was desperate for cash. I had recently left full time employment and the bills were mounting up.

My first venture as a self-employed person was selling SMS text messaging services to local businesses. In poverty-stricken desperation I had taken to walking round local shops, asking shop owners if they would like to speak to me about my services. The answer of course, was a resounding 'no'. In my wretchedness though, I persisted. Something had to happen.

One cold Tuesday morning in February I walked into a hair salon, and by chance spoke to the salon owner. I asked if I could talk to him about SMS text messaging.

"No, my accountant deals with all of my taxes, thank you," he responded.

"No no, not taxes. Text messaging", I said. "Like on your phone."

The salon owner paused for a moment. "Well", he said, "I don't think I need that. But can you get me to the top of Google? You know, in the Google rankings?"

A week later I was back, armed with my ageing laptop. We perched on a bench in the hair salon. Three yards away a customer was having her hair blow dried.

The salon owner had brought along his business associate for the 'meeting', who hovered nervously around the edge of the bench. I quickly demonstrated the website I had mocked up in WordPress.

"That's very nice," said the salon owner. "So how much is it going to cost?"

I let out a slow breath. "Well, it's going to be about seven hours. So £300."

"£300!" exclaimed the owner. "No no no. That's far too much. I've had quotes in the past for £100."

I shuffled on the bench for a moment. I glanced from the owner, to his suddenly serious-looking associate. Sod it, what the hell.

"Fine, I'll do it!"

A week or so later the tagline on my website 'Rob Drummond, SMS text messaging expert' had been replaced by 'Rob Drummond, web designer.' A friend who worked locally as a photographer suggested I email some of the local networking groups. I found a group that met nearby at 7AM on Thursday mornings.

A few hours later Richard from the networking group emailed me back. 'We're very sorry Rob, but we already have a web designer in the group. We'd be very happy to meet you though in another capacity.'

I thought about this for an evening. I remembered the salon owner's excitement at the thought of appearing 'in the Google rankings'. Finally, I scratched out 'Rob Drummond, web designer', and pencilled in 'Rob Drummond, Google AdWords expert'. I ordered 100 business cards, and told Richard I'd be along the following week.

The first meeting I went to was mildly terrifying. Somehow, I managed to talk about my budding yet non-existent AdWords business without being exposed as a fraud.

Over the following months I had some initial success talking about AdWords. My client roster was clocking up nicely. Money issues had faded. I even managed to successfully run my own ads bidding on the phrase match term "google adwords". And yet, there was a problem.

Something didn't feel right. The money in AdWords lies in managing big accounts at scale. I knew how to do that. But it didn't really... feel like me.

I've always maintained my own email list. I've always written at least one weekly email. One day a client remarked, "you're pretty good at these emails Rob. How much would you charge for a short email series?"

The problem with being *reasonably* good at a range of marketing skills is you easily get pulled in different directions. I was managing Google AdWords accounts. I was creating web pages. I was working on email sequences. I was creating Google Analytics dashboards. I ended up acting as an outsourced marketing department for clients who didn't really have the budget to pay for it.

Business still wasn't great. A few friends and family members had 'hinted' that I ought to put my toys back in the box, and get a real job for a bit. My wife Linzi silently told me the same thing with her eyes.

This continued until March 2016, when I flew to Arizona to attend a conference. As I waited to board my flight, I remember thinking… "everybody is going to ask me what I *do*. I don't have a clear answer. *Shit*, I'm in trouble..."

I went to Arizona to network and pick up a client or two. In reality, I felt smashed by a proverbial train. I remember listening to Gary Vaynerchuk's talk in the final session. As a throw-away comment, Gary said:

"All of you who are sitting there trying to do seven different things and spin seven different plates, you need to stop. Just stop. Pick one of them you like best, and start winning."

Slam.

I came back from Arizona with a renewed purpose. I knew that storytelling in marketing was important, and I knew how little help there was. My mission now is to help people who sell transformational products to tell their story to their target audience.

It's been a long road to discover my real purpose in business, but it's been more than worth the ordeal.

(Link to content)

(Email signature)

Notes

As previously I have colour-coded the different stages below. The key section in the rags to riches plot is the central crisis, in the middle. This story would also be effective as a three-part email series, with a 'before' email, a 'central crisis' email, and an 'after' email.

Stages Walkthrough

Stage 1: Initial wretchedness and 'call'
Stage 2: Out into the world, initial success
Stage 3: The central crisis
Stage 4: Independence and final ordeal
Stage 5: Completion and fulfilment

Subject: "Can you get me to the top of Google?"

Hi ~Contact.FirstName~,

(Start of Stage 1)

In summer 2012 I was desperate for cash. I had recently left full time employment and the bills were mounting up.

My first venture as a self-employed person was selling SMS text messaging services to local businesses. In poverty-stricken desperation I had taken to walking round local shops, asking shop owners if they would like to speak to me about my services. The answer of course, was a resounding 'no'. In my wretchedness though, I persisted. Something had to happen.

(End of Stage 1)

I've included the wording 'in poverty-stricken desperation' to make stage 1 obvious to you. You can use other wording, but you should spend some time in stage 1 describing to the reader just how dejected, downtrodden or wretched you were.

(Start of Stage 2)

One cold Tuesday morning in February I walked into a hair salon, and by chance spoke to the salon owner. I asked if I could talk to him about SMS text messaging.

"No, my accountant deals with all of my taxes, thank you," he responded.

"No no, not taxes. Text messaging", I said. "Like on your phone."

The salon owner paused for a moment. "Well", he said, "I don't think I need that. But can you get me to the top of Google? You know, in the Google rankings?"

A week later I was back, armed with my ageing laptop. We perched on a bench in the hair salon. Three yards away a customer was having her hair blow dried.

The salon owner had brought along his business associate for the 'meeting', who hovered nervously around the edge of the bench. I quickly demonstrated the website I had mocked up in WordPress.

"That's very nice," said the salon owner. "So how much is it going to cost?"

I let out a slow breath. "Well, it's going to be about seven hours. So £300."

"£300!" exclaimed the owner. "No no no. That's far too much.

I've had quotes in the past for £100."

I shuffled on the bench for a moment. I glanced from the owner, to his suddenly serious-looking associate. Sod it, what the hell.

"Fine, I'll do it!"

A week or so later the tagline on my website 'Rob Drummond, SMS text messaging expert' had been replaced by 'Rob Drummond, web designer.' A friend who worked locally as a photographer suggested I email some of the local networking groups. I found a group that met nearby at 7AM on Thursday mornings.

A few hours later Richard from the networking group emailed me back. 'We're very sorry Rob, but we already have a web designer in the group. We'd be very happy to meet you though in another capacity.'

I thought about this for an evening. I remembered the salon owner's excitement at the thought of appearing 'in the Google rankings'. Finally, I scratched out 'Rob Drummond, web designer', and pencilled in 'Rob Drummond, Google AdWords expert'. I ordered 100 business cards, and told Richard I'd be along the following week.

The first meeting I went to was mildly terrifying. Somehow, I managed to talk about my budding yet non-existent AdWords business without being exposed as a fraud.

Over the following months I had some initial success talking about AdWords. My client roster was clocking up nicely. Money issues had faded. I even managed to successfully run my own ads bidding on the phrase match term "google adwords". And yet, there was a problem.

(End of Stage 2)

—

In stage 2, you show the hero of the story (probably you) as having some initial success, but perhaps achieving it by putting on a 'front', rather than acting as their 'real self'.

—

(Start of Stage 3)

Something didn't feel right. The money in AdWords lies in managing big accounts at scale. I knew how to do that. But it didn't really... feel like me.

I've always maintained my own email list. I've always written at least one weekly email. One day a client remarked, "you're pretty good at these emails Rob. How much would you charge for a short email series?"

The problem with being *reasonably* good at a range of marketing skills is you easily get pulled in different directions. I was managing Google AdWords accounts. I was creating web pages. I was working on email sequences. I was creating Google Analytics dashboards. I ended up acting as an outsourced marketing department for clients who didn't really have the budget to pay for it.

Business still wasn't great. A few friends and family members had 'hinted' that I ought to put my toys back in the box, and get a real job for a bit. My wife Linzi silently told me the same thing with her eyes.

(End of Stage 3)

The central crisis is the crux of the story. Here, you normally want to introduce some reflective conflict. Give your readers an insight into the dilemma playing out in your head.

(Start of Stage 4)

This continued until March 2016, when I flew to Arizona to attend a conference. As I waited to board my flight, I remember thinking… "everybody is going to ask me what I *do*. I don't have a clear answer. *Shit*, I'm in trouble…"

I went to Arizona to network and pick up a client or two. In reality, I felt smashed by a proverbial train. I remember listening to Gary Vaynerchuk's talk in the final session. As a throw-away comment, Gary said:

"If you're trying to do seven different things and spin seven different plates, you need to stop. Just stop. Pick one of them you like best, and start winning."

Slam.

(End of Stage 4)

At the final ordeal, you need to show your reader how you finally 'saw the light'. Show them how you were finally able to do things your way, and stand alone on your own two feet.

(Start of Stage 5)

I came back from Arizona with a renewed purpose. I knew that storytelling in marketing was important, and I knew how little help there was. My mission now is to help people who sell transformational products to tell their story to their target audience.

It's been a long road to discover my real purpose in business, but it's been more than worth the ordeal.

(End of Stage 5)

Stage 5 illustrates the new you. You should display your riches here. 'Riches' could mean a richer experience, a richer perspective, a richer purpose, or indeed material wealth.

3. The Quest

The quest involves a physical journey to an unfamiliar far-away place, accompanied by a number of helpers. *The Lord of the Rings*, *Homer's Iliad*, *Indiana Jones* and *Shrek* are all examples of the quest plot.

The quest plot harks back to a time of nomadic human development, when moving around into strange and unfamiliar territory was a regular part of human life. The human origin story, or the 'out of Africa' theory described earlier, is essentially a quest. The 16th century expeditions to the 'New World' were all quests. Any time you travel alone in a 'developing' part of the world, you are inadvertently throwing yourself into a 'quest'.

The hero of a quest will normally have one or more companions. (A sceptical reader might argue that a quest with no companions and no dialogue would be a rather dull read!)

The quest is the first plot we have looked at where the main hero and his companions all display their flaws openly in the story. Usually the characters on the quest will possess different skills and abilities, allowing different members of the quest party to save the day in difficult moments.

At 'relief points' in the quest there will often be light characters, or helpers. The light characters are unable to impact the outcome of the story, but provide relief and recuperation after a period of pressure. In *The Lord of the Rings*, Arwen and Elrond provide relief from the dark riders in Rivendell.

The stages in the quest plot are:

1. The call

The need for the quest becomes urgently apparent. The hero of the quest will be forced quickly into action. Frodo is forced to flee The Shire. Shrek's swamp is filled with fairytale creatures.

2. The journey

We see the pattern of constriction and expansion throughout the journey, where pressure on the companions from dark forces is increased and released. This emotional rollercoaster is essential to maintain interest in the journey. Perhaps surprisingly, the journey part of the quest rarely takes up the entire story.

3. Arrival and frustration

Halfway through *The Lord of the Rings*, Frodo and his companions are already close to Mordor. The real challenge however is getting *into* Mordor. Close to the point of completion, the hero will be frustratingly held up, perhaps waylaid by a devilish temptress.

In the 1986 film *Labyrinth*, Sarah makes it most of the way to the Goblin King's castle before being held up by Hoggle's poisonous peach.

4. The final ordeal

After being frustratingly held up, our hero will fight one or a series of battles with the dark force of the story (there can be up to three). Often there will be an impossible choice for the hero to make. James Bond must invariably choose between saving the girl, or saving the world.

5. The goal

The story ends with dark forces repelled, and a great renewal of life centred on a new, more secure base.

How to translate this into a business story

The point of the quest story is less about the quest itself, and more about the character change the hero must go through to complete the quest.

Your use of the quest plot will really depend on how much you travel. If your work involves plenty of travel in less-frequently visited parts of the world, you'll have more raw material for potential quest stories.

The quest must involve a physical journey, and there must be obstacles or temptations along the way. Writing about your 'quest' to the beaches of the Bahamas is not an interesting read.

The quest is very relevant if your core product involves some sort of journey, trip or expedition. If that describes your business the quest will become your main archetypal plot.

Potential use cases for the quest include:

- Travel nightmares
- Trips, journeys or expeditions
- Visiting a customer
- Running a trade show (or similar event)

Quest Example

Subject: ¡A la esquina por favor!

Hi ~Contact.FirstName~,

On 1st August 2009 I stood on the salt flats of Uyuni; one of the driest places on earth.

I almost didn't get there.

The Salar De Uyuni is in south west Bolivia, and formed millions of years ago when two prehistoric lakes dried out. A crusty metre-thick layer of salt now covers over 4,086 square miles.

I woke up the previous day in the city of Sucre. Sucre isn't far from Uyuni by Bolivian standards, but is still a 12-hour bus journey over largely unmade roads. I had to change buses half way in the mining city of Potosí.

I arrived at the bus terminal in Sucre six hours before my connecting bus. Sucre to Potosí is a popular journey. Women around the gates of the terminal were frantically selling bus tickets, trilling a high pitch "PotosíPotosíPotosí! Potosí ahora!"

I bought a ticket and embarked on a brisk walk to the apparently soon-to-depart bus. Bay four. As I rounded the corner I saw the bus was deserted, with no driver and the engine off.

I sat on the bus ready to go, watching the minutes tick past. Bus departure times in Bolivia are arbitrary and subject to ticket sales, driver sobriety, wind direction and various other factors.

Eventually a driver turned up chewing coca leaves. A few other people wandered on board. "Vamos maestro!" Someone shouted. With a slow 'chug chug chug' the ancient engine spluttered into life. I glanced at my watch. Still plenty of time to make the connection.

As we pulled out of the terminal gates heading in the opposite direction to Potosí, tinny Bolivian pop music began to blare out from hidden speakers. For an hour and a half, we drove in circles around town collecting more passengers. I glanced at my watch, and stared at the seat in front of me. I was running out of time.

With the sun setting high over the Andes, we finally set off up the highway. The road to Potosí rises 1,200 metres. At times we dropped to little more than walking speed, the ancient engine roaring in second gear.

Buses in Bolivia stop anywhere for anyone, whatever they are carrying. Every mile or two we would stop in the Andean wilderness to pick up another woman waiting with a HUGE sack of corn, five children and some chickens. Two minutes later she would want to get off, prompting a jovial cry of "¡Esquina! ¡A la esquina por favor!" (at the corner please).

There was no corner to stop at, but that doesn't matter when you're the only passenger on the bus in a hurry.

After six hours of runaway chickens and Bolivian party music, we pulled up in Potosí. The lit-up outline of the Cerro Rico mountain dominated the dark skyline. Needless to say, I had missed my connecting bus. No more Uyuni buses until tomorrow.

I thought briefly about cutting my losses and heading to a hostel. I knew a decent enough place to stay in Potosí, and a decent enough bar too.

But no. I had a salt flat tour booked to leave tomorrow morning from Uyuni, and tomorrow was the only day I could do it. Perhaps ever. It had to be tomorrow.

Many big cities in Bolivia have shared taxi services running between them. A few taxi drivers were standing near the bus terminal, trilling "Sucre! Sucre! Seis Bolivianos a Sucre!" If it cost six Bolivianos to get back to Sucre in a shared taxi, I wondered how much it would cost to get to Uyuni by myself. I went up and asked.

The question caused a brief silence among the taxi people. The woman in front of me looked at me questioningly. "Uyuni? Hoy?"

"Hoy." I said. Today.

After a moment's reflection, she came up with a number. "Mil quinientos", she said. One thousand five hundred. 1,500 Bolivianos is about £130, or $200. To put that into context, 1,500

Bolivianos is a month's wages for many Bolivians.

I tried to bargain, but they weren't moving. Fifteen hundred Bolivianos it was. I shoved my bag into the back of a taxi under the watchful eye of a suspicious looking taxi driver. We stopped at a cash machine, then set off.

The road from Potosí to Uyuni is barely a road. Huge craters litter the surface, like the moon.

My overwhelming feeling as I sat there in the car was regret, intermingled with fear. Fear that I didn't really know where I was going. Fear that I had decided to ride alone into a desert with two strangers, with a stupidly large amount of money in my pocket.

At three in the morning we finally arrived at Uyuni. I paid my driver, and exited the car before he had finished counting the money.

Uyuni at night is unlit, bitterly cold, and stray dogs patrol the streets. I could hear dogs howling nearby. I scurried into the first hotel with lights on.

Was the quest worth it? I would say so. Uyuni is one of the most distinctive places I have ever been. It never rains, and miles of vast white expanse extend as far as you can see.

(Link to content)

(Email signature)

Notes

I've included a personal example of a 'quest' story here, rather than a business example. There is no reason why you cannot include personal stories in your emails, as long as you successfully reconnect to your content.

In the example, where I have finished with '(Link to content)', I could explain how I got to Uyuni *in spite* of my terrible decisions. Terrible decisions would then provide the link to my content. I might for example begin my content by explaining how many people make terrible decisions when they select a copywriter, or an email marketing platform.

Stages Walkthrough

Stage 1: The call
Stage 2: The journey
Stage 3: Arrival and frustration
Stage 4: The final ordeal
Stage 5: The goal

Subject: ¡A la esquina por favor!

Hi ~Contact.FirstName~,

(Start of Stage 1)

On 1st August 2009 I stood on the salt flats of Uyuni; one of the driest places on earth.

I almost didn't get there.

The Salar De Uyuni is in south west Bolivia, and formed millions of years ago when two prehistoric lakes dried out. A crusty metre-thick layer of salt now covers over 4,086 square miles.

Sucre isn't far from Uyuni by Bolivian standards, but is still a 12-hour bus journey over largely unmade roads. I had to change buses half way in the mining city of Potosí.

I arrived at the bus terminal in Sucre six hours before my connecting bus. Sucre to Potosí is a popular journey. Women around the gates of the terminal were frantically selling bus tickets, trilling a high pitch "PotosíPotosíPotosí! Potosí ahora!"

(End of Stage 1)

At stage 1 the need for the quest should normally become urgently apparent. In this case however I have described how I set off on the quest at a leisurely pace, unaware of the imminent time pressure.

(Start of Stage 2)

I bought a ticket and embarked on a brisk walk to the apparently soon-to-depart bus. Bay four. As I rounded the corner I saw the bus was deserted, with no driver and the engine off.

I sat on the bus ready to go, watching the minutes tick past. Bus departure times in Bolivia are arbitrary and subject to ticket sales, driver sobriety, wind direction and various other factors.

Eventually a driver turned up chewing coca leaves. A few other people wandered on board. "Vamos maestro!" Someone shouted. With a slow 'chug chug chug' the ancient engine spluttered into life. I glanced at my watch. Still plenty of time to make the connection.

As we pulled out of the terminal gates heading in the opposite direction to Potosí, tinny Bolivian pop music began to blare out from hidden speakers. For an hour and a half, we drove in circles around town collecting more passengers. I glanced at my watch, and stared at the seat in front of me. I was running out of time.

With the sun setting high over the Andes, we finally set off up the highway. The road to Potosí rises 1,200 metres. At times we dropped to little more than walking speed, the ancient engine roaring in second gear.

Buses in Bolivia stop anywhere for anyone, whatever they are carrying. Every mile or two we would stop in the Andean wilderness to pick up another woman waiting with a HUGE sack of corn, five children and some chickens. Two minutes later she would want to get off, prompting a jovial cry of "¡Esquina! ¡A la esquina por favor!" (at the corner please).

There was no corner to stop at, but that doesn't matter when you're the only passenger on the bus in a hurry.

After six hours of runaway chickens and Bolivian party music, we pulled up in Potosí. The lit-up outline of the Cerro Rico mountain dominated the dark skyline. Needless to say, I had missed my connecting bus. No more Uyuni buses until tomorrow.

(End of Stage 2)

The journey should toy with your emotions. At some points I think we'll make it in time. At other points I can only watch the seat in front of me in despair.

(Start of Stage 3)

I thought briefly about cutting my losses and heading to a hostel. I knew a decent enough place to stay in Potosí, and a decent enough bar too.

But no. I had a salt flat tour booked to leave tomorrow morning from Uyuni, and tomorrow was the only day I could do it. Perhaps ever. It had to be tomorrow.

Many big cities in Bolivia have shared taxi services running between them. A few taxi drivers were standing near the bus terminal, trilling "Sucre! Sucre! Seis Bolivianos a Sucre!" If it cost six Bolivianos to get back to Sucre in a shared taxi, I wondered how much it would cost to get to Uyuni by myself. I went up and asked.

The question caused a brief silence among the taxi people. The woman in front of me looked at me questioningly. "Uyuni? Hoy?"

"Hoy." I said. Today.

After a moment's reflection, she came up with a number. "Mil quinientos", she said. One thousand five hundred. 1,500 Bolivianos is about £130, or $200. To put that into context, 1,500 Bolivianos is a month's wages for many Bolivians.

(End of Stage 3)

The 'arrival' in this story is actually in Potosí, not Uyuni. Notice how I dwelt on my frustration, and thought about heading to a bar. The frustration part of the story is a good place to introduce reflective conflict.

(Start of Stage 4)

I tried to bargain, but they weren't moving. Fifteen hundred Bolivianos it was. I shoved my bag into the back of a taxi under the watchful eye of a suspicious looking taxi driver. We stopped at a cash machine, then set off.

The road from Potosí to Uyuni is barely a road. Huge craters litter the surface, like the moon.

My overwhelming feeling as I sat there in the car was regret, intermingled with fear. Fear that I didn't really know where I was going. Fear that I had decided to ride alone into a desert with two strangers, with a stupidly large amount of money in my pocket.

At three in the morning we finally arrived at Uyuni. I paid my driver, and exited the car before he had finished counting the money.

Uyuni at night is unlit, bitterly cold, and stray dogs patrol the streets. I could hear dogs howling nearby. I scurried into the first hotel with lights on.

(End of Stage 4)

The 'final ordeal' should feel hopeless at some points. In this example, the real ordeal was with myself. Wrestling with my own decision making, and questioning whether I had made the right choice.

(Start of Stage 5)

Was the quest worth it? I would say so. Uyuni is one of the most distinctive places I have ever been. It never rains here, and miles of vast white expanse extend as far as you can see.

(End of Stage 5)

The quest should always end with the goal being achieved, and lessons being learned on the way.

4. Comedy

The word comedy in modern times evokes the idea of frivolous entertainment or hilarity, but this definition of comedy is very modern. If you study a Shakespeare comedy such as *Twelfth*

Night you'll find sections of humour, but the humour is not the main point of the story.

The point of the comedy plot is the interaction between two or more characters who don't quite see clearly. In some way, the characters are blinded or unable to see the true reality of their situation. At the end, everything comes together in a single clarifying event to provide our happy ending. In *Pride and Prejudice,* Mr Darcy and Elizabeth Bennet do eventually run off into the sunset.

You can use the comedy plot in your nurture emails without anyone ever realising they are reading 'comedy', because what you are writing probably won't be fall-off-your-chair funny.

The most notable feature of comedy is the obscuring of identities. The chief characters will likely be blind to the true identity of either themselves or the other characters. This creates confusion, which must be untangled for the story to come to a happy conclusion. We as the audience can see the true nature of the situation, which creates the humour.

The comic masks of ancient Greece were ugly and distorted, but not in pain. The 'dark force' in the comedy plot comes from confusion and uncertainty over identity. From characters putting on a distorted 'front', and not showing up as their real selves.

The stages in the comedy plot are:

1. Pass into confusion, uncertainty and frustration

In the confusion, key characters become shut off from one another. The 'dark force' in comedy is confusion.

2. The dream stage

The plot may seem to resolve, but something still isn't right. The key characters are still not seeing things for what they really are.

In *War and Peace*, Natasha falls for the charming tempter, Anatole Kuragin, but quickly realises she has made a mistake.

3. The nightmarish tangle

The confusion worsens. We often see characters going into the 'lower' world, to try and discover who they really are. In *War and Peace*, Pierre goes to the front line of the war with France.

The nightmarish tangle can never be resolved by the main characters staying happily at home. Some kind of harrowing experience in a 'lower' domain is usually required to get to stage 4.

4. The event of clarity

On his war-weary travels, Pierre meets Platon Karataev, a Russian peasant. Through his interaction with Platon, Pierre finally understands what he has been seeking; an honest person with no hidden agenda.

At the event of clarity, the nightmarish tangle is finally resolved. In the nick of time, key characters finally begin to see each other for who they really are.

5. Resolution

The confusion is finally resolved. Comedy always ends with a joyful reunion, which in turn leads to a renewal of life. In a business story this could translate to a renewal of purpose or energy.

How to translate this into a business story

The comedy plot requires a degree of humility to work. The comedy plot focuses on your confusion about a particular situation, and about your relationship with other characters. Exposing yourself as imperfect makes you vulnerable, but the vulnerability allows your readers to connect with the story.

Common uses for comedy include:

- Confusions about roles
- Customer misunderstandings
- Supplier misunderstandings
- Office romances

I remember Perry Marshall talking about the time he offered to give away 1,500 MacBooks at an event, only to discover it was impossible to get hold of that many on credit. There was a happy resolution to the story, but he almost killed himself in the process.

Comedy Example

Subject: I @$#ing do email marketing!

Hi ~Contact.FirstName~,

In 2013 I did an AdWords project for a client named Brian*.

Brian was in a B2B market, where the sales cycle was potentially long. Beyond the initial flurry of follow-up from his overly-aggressive telesales team, most of his leads were left to go cold. Brian wasn't sure which leads were converting into business.

At the very beginning of the project I had suggested that AdWords was only part of the solution he needed. I thought there was a big opportunity to build out an automated email sequence. I mentioned it once or twice, and eventually left it with him. At the time, Brian wasn't convinced that an email follow-up sequence would deliver the results he wanted.

In the following weeks, Brian's AdWords results showed a steady improvement. Cost per conversion dropped to within an acceptable level. After two months, Brian sent me an email.

"Hi Rob. As per your suggestion I've set up a Mailchimp account. I've also hired [so-and-so] to write the emails for me."

I can't remember what so-and-so's name was, but I can remember I almost popped a vein.

"Brian I @$#ing do email marketing!" I yelled at the email.

Later on when I had calmed down and got him on the phone, Brian remarked, "I didn't realise you did that. I thought you were just the AdWords guy."

Just the AdWords guy. Pfft.

Anyhow, so-and-so eventually got to work on the emails. The popped vein in my forehead had just about healed over by the time I got to read the fruits of so-and-so's labours. The opening email began:

'At XYZ, we believe...'

Any time you start a marketing email with 'at our company we believe' a small part of me dies on the inside and withers away.

The email then proceeded to talk in tired clichés about levels of service and customer care. The last emails in the series were little more than reminders. I asked Brian what sort of brief he had provided to so-and-so.

"Oh, I just sent him to the website. It's all on there."

No wonder the emails were crap.

Despite the questionable quality of the emails, the initial sequence had convinced Brian that email marketing was a viable way to close sales. I went to see him for an afternoon, and we mapped out exactly what each email ought to say, and how it would generate more leads for the sales team.

Eventually he asked how much it would cost for me to rewrite his emails, although I think he still harboured a little suspicion about letting the *AdWords guy* loose on his emails.

(Link to content)

(Email signature)

*Name changed for privacy.

Notes

A comedy plot always centres around some confusion over identity. The comedy plot is highly flexible, and lends itself to shorter stories. An element of comedy can often be woven into another plot, as we saw in the Rags to Riches example.

Stages Walkthrough

Stage 1: Pass into confusion, uncertainty and frustration
Stage 2: The dream stage
Stage 3: The nightmarish tangle
Stage 4: The event of clarity
Stage 5: Resolution

Subject: I @$#ing do email marketing!

Hi ~Contact.FirstName~,

(Start of Stage 1)

In 2013 I did an AdWords project for a client named Brian.

Brian was in a B2B market, where the sales cycle was potentially long. Beyond the initial flurry of follow-up from his overly-aggressive telesales team, most of his leads were left to go cold. Brian wasn't sure which leads were converting into business.

At the very beginning of the project I had suggested that AdWords was only part of the solution he needed. I thought there was a big opportunity to build out an automated email sequence.

I mentioned it once or twice, and eventually left it with him. At the time, Brian wasn't convinced that an email follow-up sequence would deliver the results he wanted.

(End of Stage 1)

The key thing in stage 1 is to introduce some element of confusion.

(Start of Stage 2)

In the following weeks, Brian's AdWords results showed a steady improvement. Cost per conversion dropped to within an acceptable level. After two months, Brian sent me an email.

(End of Stage 2)

—

I haven't dwelt much on the dream stage here, but it is essential that you *do* have a dream stage. The dream stage sits in stark contrast to the tangle of confusion that follows.

—

(Start of Stage 3)

"Hi Rob. As per your suggestion I've set up a Mailchimp account. I've also hired [so-and-so] to write the emails for me."

I can't remember what so-and-so's name was, but I can remember I almost popped a vein.

"Brian I @$#ing do email marketing!" I yelled at the email.

Later on when I had calmed down and got him on the phone, Brian remarked, "I didn't realise you did that. I thought you were just the AdWords guy."

Just the AdWords guy. Pfft.

Anyhow, so-and-so eventually got to work on the emails. The popped vein in my forehead had just about healed over by the time I got to read the fruits of so-and-so's labours. The opening email began:

'At XYZ, we believe...'

Any time you start a marketing email with 'at our company we believe' a small part of me dies on the inside and withers away.

The email then proceeded to talk in tired clichés about levels of service and customer care. The last emails in the series were little more than reminders. I asked Brian what sort of brief he had provided to so-and-so.

"Oh, I just sent him to the website. It's all on there."

No wonder the emails were crap.

(End of Stage 3)

—

Stage 3 is the 'nightmarish tangle'. The key thing here is to take your time explaining the tangle. Showing an emotion that illustrates your frustration can also be a good idea, like me yelling at Brian's email.

—

(Start of Stage 4)

Despite the questionable quality of the emails, the initial

sequence had convinced Brian that email marketing was a viable way to close sales. I went to see him for an afternoon, and we mapped out exactly what each email ought to say, and how it would generate more leads for the sales team.

(End of Stage 4)

The 'event of clarity' is short and to the point here. You could build the 'event of clarity' out into a more drawn-out penny-dropping moment. The event of clarity is the moment the confusion finally disappears.

(Start of Stage 5)

Eventually he asked how much it would cost for me to rewrite his emails, although I think he still harboured a little suspicion about letting the *AdWords guy* loose on his emails.

(End of Stage 5)

5. Tragedy

Most business owners recoil from the idea of using tragedy in a story, not least because the first instinct of marketers is to sugar-coat any message with joy and arrogance.

Tragedy is quite similar to comedy, except that our hero has fallen too far into the clutches of evil to be redeemed in a happy finale. Death is the eventual outcome, but society at large emerges from the story better off. Macbeth dies and the kingdom of Scotland emerges from darkness.

The word 'tragedy' comes from the Greek word for 'a goat'. This is where we get the word 'scapegoat', the practice of sacrificing a goat or other animal to preserve the wider community.

Tragedy follows the same five-step format as the other archetypes, but the drama is viewed through the eyes of the main dark figure. The 'dark power' in the story resides within the main hero, rather than in another dark character or monster. In a sense the hero is also the monster.

The dark characters in tragedy are never completely dark, which is what makes their eventual downfall tragic. A tragic hero will always display obvious flaws, and grappling with these flaws in an isolated and self-centred way always leads to their eventual isolation and destruction.

In many cases the dark hero will keep their 'real self' hidden underneath a light and respectable exterior. Dexter comes to mind as an obvious example. Dexter lives by day as a respectable blood spatter analyst, and by night as a killer.

As the tragedy plot develops, we as the audience *want* the dark hero to mend his ways and reform. He may make attempts to do so, but eventually ends up killing or brutally rejecting the people around him.

The five stages look like this:

1. Anticipation or 'call'

The hero is in some way unfulfilled. His thoughts turn to the future, and some object or item of desire commands his focus. Often this could be power, money or influence.

A tragedy plot often starts with a dilemma. In the early stages of the plot there will often be a 'tempter' or 'temptress', playing on the hero's flaws and tempting him to choose the dark path. Dilemmas and choices have always been a key part of tragedy.

In the theatre of Ancient Greece, the role of tragedy was to present the audience with a dilemma. In the ancient Athenian democracy, citizens were expected to play an active role in public decisions. The plays of Aeschylus in the 5th Century BC can really be viewed as a form of social training; providing the audience with a staged dilemma, in case the real-life Persians were to show up.

(In 490BC the real Persian army did show up, and were miraculously defeated against the odds at the battle of Marathon).

2. The dream stage

The hero commits to a course of action, and for a while things go surprisingly well. For a while he seems to 'get away with it'. Macbeth seems to get away with the murder of King Duncan. Dexter seems to get away with his life as a killer.

3. Frustration stage

Almost imperceptibly, things begin to unravel. In choosing a course of action, our hero always overlooks something important. The situation becomes more complicated. Further 'dark acts' will be committed to try and rectify the situation. In doing so, the hero begins to isolate himself from the supporting characters around him.

4. Nightmare stage

Things slip completely out of control. Our hero becomes isolated from reality and other people. Macbeth ends up in an isolated, murderous state of insanity.

5. Destruction

The destruction of the tragic hero serves as a wider lesson for the community, and enables an overall renewal of life.

How to translate this into a business story

Tragedy is a great plot to use when you need your audience to stop and think.

The real role of tragedy is to highlight the dangers or downside of not working with you, or not taking up your offer. The danger could be physical, financial, or perhaps a break-down of family relationships.

If someone who needs your services decides not to take up your offer, what is the worst thing that can happen to them? Write a story about that and you have yourself a tragedy plot.

Tragedy always ends in the death of the hero, but a renewal of life overall. A tragedy plot could be about:

- The death of a person
- The death of a product
- The death of a dream
- The death of ambition
- A previous business failure (the death of a business)

Tragedy Example

To show you how a tragedy plot can be developed I'm going to share an email I rewrote for a client. The client's original email can be found in the appendix of this book.

Hey ~Contact.FirstName~,

2002, Mount Hood, Oregon. After toiling all afternoon in the weak midwinter sun, a group of nine climbers are within striking distance of the summit. One night of fame and glory are almost within sight.

The team have made good progress. Each climber is tied to another member of the party. For a while the going isn't too steep, so they don't take the time to put in any protection.

"If my partner falls," one climber thinks, "I can self arrest and stop their fall."

The climbing route becomes steeper, but half of the group don't notice. Another member thinks he can still self arrest if needed. The climber at the head of the group is mostly worried about the time. Without continued good progress, it may become too late to summit.

In a flash, one climber falls. He doesn't stop. His partner curses and gets into self arrest position. By the time the rope comes tight, the fallen climber is going about 30 miles an hour. His teammate, who is in self arrest position ostensibly to stop his climbing partner's slide, is ripped from his stance.

While falling, one rope team tangles up with a second, and then a third. Like a bad Wile E. Coyote cartoon, the group tangles up into a giant ball of yarn and hurtles down the mountain until they come to rest in a crevasse. 2 are dead. 5 more are seriously injured. The rescue helicopter, sent up in windy conditions, also crashes killing the pilot.

We use climbing ropes to make us safer. This much should be obvious. Less obvious are the several ways a rope can be used to make you safer.

You can use a traditional belay, where one climber waits at the bottom and feeds out rope to the climber. If they slip, the climber at the bottom catches her fallen friend.

You can use running protection, where both climbers climb at the same time, but clip the rope to something while they go. Here, if someone falls, you might get pulled off your stance, but the protection should hold you and save you.

You can travel in "glacier travel" mode, where you walk along, tied to someone, and if you fall, they act as your anchor.

You can short rope, where a rope is used to correct a slip before it becomes a fall.

These are all used, and are quite appropriate at various times.

Sometimes, the rope makes things more dangerous.

On a tough ascent, time is of the essence. It always is. If you belayed everything out, you'd never get anywhere. Maybe you should use running pro. Or maybe no rope at all.

Decisions, decisions…

If you were interested in mountaineering, that would be thought provoking, right? That's the point about tragedy – you learn something and it makes you think.

The five stages of the tragedy plot are:

Stage 1: Anticipation or 'call'
Stage 2: The dream stage
Stage 3: Frustration stage
Stage 4: Nightmare stage
Stage 5: Destruction

Stages Walkthrough

Hey ~Contact.FirstName~,

(Start of Stage 1)

2002, Mount Hood, Oregon. After toiling all afternoon in the weak midwinter sun, a group of nine climbers are within striking distance of the summit. One night of fame and glory are almost within sight.

(End of Stage 1)

—

Stage 1 is the anticipation, or 'call' stage. Some kind of goal or objective is introduced, in this case a night of fame and glory.

—

(Start of Stage 2)

The team have made good progress. Each climber is tied to
another member of the party. For a while the going isn't too
steep, so they don't take the time to put in any protection.

"If my partner falls," one climber thinks, "I can self arrest and
stop their fall."

(End of Stage 2)

—

Stage 2 is the dream phase. The group have selected a course of
action, and are so far making good progress. The choices they
have made seem to be paying off.

—

(Start of Stage 3)

The climbing route becomes steeper, but half of the group don't
notice. Another member thinks he can still self arrest if needed.
The climber at the head of the group is mostly worried about the
time. Without continued good progress, it may become too late
to summit.

In a flash, one climber falls. He doesn't stop. His partner curses
and gets into self arrest position. By the time the rope comes
tight, the fallen climber is going about 30 miles an hour. His
teammate, who is in self arrest position ostensibly to stop his
climbing partner's slide, is ripped from his stance.

(End of Stage 3)

In the frustration stage, things begin to go wrong. The thing that goes wrong is always avoidable, and always comes from an oversight at an earlier stage. In this particular story, the frustration stage runs quickly into the nightmare stage.

(Start of Stage 4)

While falling, one rope team tangles up with a second, and then a third. Like a bad Wile E. Coyote cartoon, the group tangles up into a giant ball of yarn and hurtles down the mountain until they come to rest in a crevasse. (End of Stage 4 / Start of Stage 5) 2 are dead. 5 more are seriously injured. The rescue helicopter, sent up in windy conditions, also crashes killing the pilot.

(End of Stage 5)

After this point, the story transitions into the content. Everything from here on in is content rather than story.

We use climbing ropes to make us safer. This much should be obvious. Less obvious are the several ways a rope can be used to make you safer.

You can use a traditional belay, where one climber waits at the bottom and feeds out rope to the climber. If they slip, the climber at the bottom catches her fallen friend.

You can use running protection, where both climbers climb at the same time, but clip the rope to something while they go. Here, if someone falls, you might get pulled off your stance, but the protection should hold you and save you.

You can travel in "glacier travel" mode, where you walk along, tied to someone, and if you fall, they act as your anchor.

You can short rope, where a rope is used to correct a slip before it becomes a fall.

These are all used, and are quite appropriate at various times. Sometimes, the rope makes things more dangerous.

On a tough ascent, time is of the essence. It always is. If you belayed everything out, you'd never get anywhere. Maybe you should use running pro. Or maybe no rope at all.

Decisions, decisions…

But isn't tragedy a bit 'Negative'?

Many people will read this book and dismiss the tragedy plot out of hand.

Most companies are too scared of the tragedy plot to use it. What I would put to you is that if you only ever send 'positive' messages to your audience, you are treating your readers like children.

Imagine that one day you are standing in your driveway, collecting today's mail. Just before you return to your house, you see a ball bounce over a fence. In a garden over the road, a small child sprints out of the house to retrieve the ball.

Just as this happens, a van rounds the corner at the top of the road, accelerating quickly. Hidden behind a hedge, there is no way the van driver can see the child. The child shows no sign of stopping, eyes fixed on the ball.

What sort of message do you shout to the child, to get his attention? Do you send a 'positive' message, encouraging him to slow down? Or do you yell a 'negative' message, warning him of the imminent danger?

You use the negative message, of course. You aren't being negative when you do this, you're just being responsible.

6. Voyage and return

Classic voyage and return stories include *Alice in Wonderland, Back to the Future, Gone with the Wind,* and *The Wizard of Oz.*

The essence of the voyage and return plot is that the hero will travel out of their familiar, normal 'everyday' surroundings, into another world completely cut off from the first. Often the story will begin with the hero somehow 'bored', or otherwise unfulfilled. They must be in an initial 'exposed' state of mind that exposes them to the possibility of the voyage.

In many voyage and return stories the voyage is set out upon by accident. In *The Lion, The Witch and The Wardrobe,* Lucy accidentally wanders through the back of her wardrobe to discover Narnia. Dorothy has her house blown away by a tornado in *The Wizard of Oz.* Marty McFly inadvertently winds up in 1955 in *Back to the Future.*

At first, the new destination will seem strange and novel. But as time goes on, the novelty begins to wear off, slowly turning into a nightmare. In every voyage and return story the real challenge is getting back. It is the experience of getting back which provides the story with its moral.

The most effective voyage and return stories are the ones where the hero must go through a personal transformation to return home. Marty McFly has to grow up and act as a 'Dad' to his own father before he can return home. Voyage and return is about developing awareness, and questioning what you know. The plot is about moving from ignorance to knowledge, and getting yourself through a sticky situation along the way.

The five stages in the plot are:

1. Anticipation and fall into the 'other world'

The hero of the story will usually start off in some kind of ego-centric boredom. Wrapped up in their own personal unhappiness, they fall into the voyage almost by accident.

2. Initial fascination or dream stage

The hero will initially be fascinated by the strangeness of his new surroundings. Things appear to be going well.

3. Frustration stage

The initial beguiling promise fades away, and the experience becomes distinctly unpleasant. Alice realises that Wonderland isn't such fun, after all.

4. Nightmare stage

It becomes obvious that getting back is a much harder task than first thought. The experience worsens into a full-on nightmare. The strangeness of the new surroundings removes some crucial defining point for the hero's sense of reality, identity and perspective. To get home, he must go through a complete psychological shift to achieve his goal.

This psychological shift away from egocentricity is the real point of the story.

5. Thrilling escape and return

The hero completes his psychological shift in the nick of time, finally returning home. They return to their initial surroundings a changed or different person. Suddenly they now value family relationships, and are now no longer solely concerned with their own personal happiness. Harmony is restored.

How to translate this into a business story

Sometimes voyage and return will be a physical journey, but the voyage and return plot could equally be a social journey, or a journey into a market.

Has there ever been a time when you accidentally got into a market, perhaps against your better judgement, and had to work hard to get back to your core business? That's voyage and return.

Have you ever opened up shop in a location that in hindsight was never appropriate?

Have you ever become involved in a social circle, and struggled to 'get out'?

Voyage and return examples could include:

- Any time you have taken a job that turned out to not be what you thought
- A poor choice of market / market niche
- A poor choice of business location
- Any times you have followed a short-term opportunity that caused you to depart from your core purpose
- Any times you mistakenly became involved in a group or community

Voyage and Return Example

Hi ~Contact.FirstName~,

In July 2009 I needed to get from Buenos Aires to Sucre, in Bolivia. I had two weeks to get there. One of the routes available to me passed through Paraguay.

"Nobody goes to Paraguay," I was advised. "There isn't much to see there." Still, I was intrigued. Away from the beaten tourist path, it sounded like an interesting ride.

I arrived over the border from Argentina into the city of Ciudad del Este. Ciudad del Este is a city of never-ending shopping mayhem. Vehicles, people and stuff were everywhere. Buses, trucks and cars careened round sharp corners, strapped to the brim with boxes. Men carrying flat screen televisions filled the streets. I successfully dodged through the crowds, got my passport stamped, and bought a Paraguayan *chipa* from a lady in the street; a sort of cheesy breakfast bread.

My plan after elbowing my way to a hotel was to somehow get to the Itaipu dam. Built in the 1980's at enormous environmental cost, it was allegedly possible to visit the dam on a local bus. After studying the map in my trusty *Footprint* guide, it seemed the bus I needed departed from just around the corner.

I arrived at the bus departure point on a street packed with buses. Buses in most South American cities do not contain place names, and will just display a single letter or number in the front window. There is no information, no map, and certainly no timetable.

I began to flag down random buses. "Vas a Itaipu?" I asked. (Are you going to Itaipu?) Bus driver after bus driver simply looked at me blankly. There were thousands of people in Ciudad del Este, and every one of them seemed to know where they were going except me.

Next I began to stop people on the street. I thought, given my primitive Spanish, that I had figured out how to ask the right question. I stopped perhaps 20 people, and asked, "De dónde sale el autobús a Itaipu?" (Do you know from where the bus to Itaipu leaves?)

Blank face after blank face. Dejected, I started the short walk back to the hotel. Just before I turned off the street I stopped one final man. The man's brow furrowed for a moment as I repeated the work 'Itaipu'.

"Ah", he said, "ItaipU!"

"Si, ItaipU!" I said. With a minor pronunciation difference that was what I had been saying the whole damn time. Excitedly, the man pointed down the road to a point not 50 yards from where I had started. "Autobús E", he revealed to me.

Eventually I boarded Autobus E, and made it to the dam. All I can tell you about the dam is it is huge. The dam is so big they run a shuttle-bus for tourists, from one side to the other.

Now you would expect, me having gone to all that trouble to uncover the identity of Autobus E, that Autobus E going the other way would simply drop me off where I got on.

You would think that, and you would be wrong.

I got *back* on Autobus E, and after 20 minutes we stopped at a busy bus terminal. I had no idea where I was. Everybody got off and the driver stopped the engine. As I studied the tiny map in my *Footprint* guide, a sinking feeling mushroomed at the base of my stomach.

I was utterly lost.

A number of motorcycle taxis were parked near the terminal. I approached clutching my *Footprint* map, which showed the location of my hotel. The bike riders took turns to look at my map. A few spun it round in their hands. Not only did the people of Paraguay speak a weird pidgin Spanish, I would later learn, but nobody seemed to have ever seen a map before.

Eventually one of the riders gestured to get on. "Vamos gringo!" he said encouragingly. Tentatively I climbed on the back of the bike.

It turned out he had no idea where I wanted to go. We rode around Ciudad del Este while he asked his buddies if any of them could read a map, and if anyone knew the mysterious location of my hotel. It started to get dark.

As we rode around, I had a nasty thought. *I'm riding around an unfamiliar city, with my passport, credit cards, and ALL of my money. This could go horribly wrong...*

Finally, after much map-spinning, a man in spectacles finally recognised the location of my hotel. My adventure back cost me $20, and a bumpy thirty minutes on the back of a motorbike.

(Connect to content)

(Email signature)

Notes

I've opted to show you a physical voyage and return here, but I could easily have written about a social voyage and return, or a voyage and return into a particular business market.

The destination in a voyage and return is usually of only marginal importance. The voyage and return plot about is the experience the main character gains from the ordeals of return.

In the first stage I exposed myself to the voyage, due to my head-strong determination to veer away from the beaten tourist track.

The five stages in the voyage and return plot are:

Stage 1: Anticipation or 'call'
Stage 2: The dream stage
Stage 3: Frustration stage
Stage 4: Nightmare stage
Stage 5: Destruction

Stages Walkthrough

(Start of Stage 1)

In July 2009 I needed to get from Buenos Aires to Sucre, in Bolivia. I had two weeks to get there. One of the routes available to me passed through Paraguay.

"Nobody goes to Paraguay," I was advised. "There isn't much to see there." Still, I was intrigued. Away from the beaten tourist path, it sounded like an interesting ride.

(End of Stage 1)

Stage 1 in voyage and return often starts with some kind of short-sighted boredom. I was bored of the main tourist routes, and wanted something more adventurous. I exposed myself to the possibility of the voyage by showing my naivety.

(Start of Stage 2)

I arrived over the border from Argentina into the city of Ciudad del Este. Ciudad del Este is a city of never-ending shopping mayhem. Vehicles, people and stuff were everywhere. Buses, trucks and cars careened round sharp corners, strapped to the brim with boxes. Men carrying flat screen televisions filled the streets. I successfully dodged through the crowds, got my passport stamped, and bought a Paraguayan chipa from a lady in the street; a sort of cheesy breakfast bread.

(End of Stage 2)

For a while, everything is strange and intriguing. I successfully buy a cheesy breakfast bread.

(Start of Stage 3)

My plan after elbowing my way to a hotel was to somehow get

to the Itaipu dam. Built in the 1980's at enormous environmental cost, it was allegedly possible to visit the dam on a local bus. After studying the map in my trusty *Footprint* guide, it seemed the bus I needed departed from just around the corner.

I arrived at the bus departure point on a street packed with buses. Buses in most South American cities do not contain place names, and will just display a single letter or number in the front window. There is no information, no map, and certainly no timetable.

I began to flag down random buses. "Vas a Itaipu?" I asked. (Are you going to Itaipu?) Bus driver after bus driver simply looked at me blankly. There were thousands of people in Ciudad del Este, and every one of them seemed to know where they were going except me.

Next I began to stop people on the street. I thought, given my primitive Spanish, that I had figured out how to ask the right question. I stopped perhaps 20 people, and asked "De dónde sale el autobús a Itaipu?" (Do you know from where the bus to Itaipu leaves?)

Blank face after blank face. Dejected, I started the short walk back to the hotel. Just before I turned off the street I stopped one final man. The man's brow furrowed for a moment as I repeated the work 'Itaipu'.

"Ah", he said, "ItaipU!"

"Si, ItaipU!" I said. With a minor pronunciation difference that was what I had been saying the whole damn time. Excitedly, the man pointed down the road to a point not 50 yards from where I had started. "Autobús E", he revealed to me.

(End of Stage 3)

The frustration stage. The novelty of the new surroundings has worn off. A key idea in the frustration stage is that all regular points of reference are removed. Not only is finding the right bus almost impossible, even asking where the bus departs from is traumatic.

--

Eventually I boarded Autobus E, and made it to the dam. All I can tell you about the dam is it is huge. The dam is so big they run a shuttle-bus for tourists, from one side to the other.

(Start of Stage 4)

Now you would expect, me having gone to all that trouble to uncover the identity of Autobus E, that Autobus E going the other way would simply drop me off where I got on.

You would think that, and you would be wrong.

I got *back* on Autobus E, and after 20 minutes we stopped at a busy bus terminal. I had no idea where I was. Everybody got off and the driver stopped the engine. As I studied the tiny map in my *Footprint* guide, a sinking feeling mushroomed at the base of my stomach.

I was utterly lost.

A number of motorcycle taxis were parked near the terminal. I approached clutching my *Footprint* map, which showed the location of my hotel. The bike riders took turns to look at my map. A few spun it round in their hands. Not only did the people of Paraguay speak a weird pidgin Spanish, I would later learn, but nobody seemed to have ever seen a map before.

Eventually one of the riders gestured to get on. "Vamos gringo!" he said encouragingly. Tentatively I climbed on the back of the bike.

It turned out he had no idea where I wanted to go. We rode around Ciudad del Este while he asked his buddies if any of them could read a map, and if anyone knew the mysterious location of my hotel. It started to get dark.

As we rode around, I had a nasty thought. *I'm riding around an unfamiliar city, with my passport, credit cards, and ALL of my money. This could go horribly wrong...*

(End of Stage 4)

The nightmare stage should implicate you in a degree of personal danger. You then escape from this personal danger in stage 5.

(Start of Stage 5)

Finally, after much map-spinning, a man in spectacles finally recognised the location of my hotel. My adventure back cost me $20, and a bumpy thirty minutes on the back of a motorbike.

(End of Stage 5)

7. Rebirth

The rebirth plot is where a major event in the story forces the main character to change their ways, often becoming a better person. Examples of rebirth stories are *Beauty and the Beast, Despicable Me, A Christmas Carol, Sleeping Beauty*.

In some respects rebirth is similar to tragedy. We see the hero of the story become seduced by some dark power or temptation, and trapped in a state of darkness. Scrooge is trapped in his dark, self-centred tendencies before his transformation. The difference with rebirth is the hero is finally saved from the 'dark spell' in a life-changing transformation.

Rebirth is about the trial and renewal of life and purpose. You might consider it a core feature of human existence.

The five stages in the rebirth plot are:

1. Young hero or heroine falls under the spell of a dark power

In the opening stage, our hero will always in some way be immature, or possess a limited state of awareness. It is this limited awareness that exposes them to the dark power. In a business context, this could mean following the wrong people, or following a path incongruent with your real self.

2. Dream stage

Things appear to go well for the hero, although often the hero will pursue his goal in the wrong way. Scrooge achieves business success, but achieves his success in a negative way. In *Sleeping Beauty*, it seems that Maleficent's threat will not come to pass as all the needles in the kingdom are destroyed.

3. Entrapment

The darkness encroaches again, revealing its full power by trapping the hero in his 'dark ways', or in a suspended state of darkness.

4. The state of entrapment continues

It seems like the dark power will win. The state of entrapment continues. Often there will be a number of failed 'rescue' attempts. Before the three ghosts appear, Bob Cratchit tries appealing to Scrooge's generosity, and is brutally rejected.

5. Miraculous redemption by a 'light' character, and reunion

Scrooge is finally 'redeemed' by Tiny Tim. In Despicable *Me*, Gru is 'redeemed' by the girls. The hero makes the switch from darkness to light, and discovers some deeper aspect of his personality he wasn't previously aware of. His eyes are in some way opened, enabling him to see the world from a new, non-selfish perspective.

How to translate this into a business story

Rebirth is a before and after plot about personal transformation. A rebirth plot could be about the 'rebirth' of your business, but more often it will be a major discovery of purpose and the events that led to that discovery.

The best rebirth stories come from a discovery of purpose rather than a change in job. To come up with a rebirth story for business use you must have undergone a dramatic change in purpose at some point in your career.

You might have one or two rebirth stories you place at the crux of the narrative that surrounds your company. Stories could be:

- Change in business direction

- Discovering (or developing) your business purpose
- A mid-life crisis

The best rebirth stories end with a refocusing and renewal of purpose. The story is about the personal transformation you had to go through to achieve that renewal.

Rebirth Example

Subject: Finding your way

Hi ~Contact.FirstName~,

A lot of people talk about going through a 'mid-life crisis'. What nobody tells you when growing up is there is also another crisis in life to endure. The 'mid-twenties crisis'.

In my early twenties I consumed as much marketing information as I could take on. I followed all of the 'gurus'. I studied web design, copywriting, SEO and PPC. I managed to know it all, while at the same time achieving little.

In 2007 I decided to put my infinite wisdom to some use, and accepted a marketing job with a small software company. At the company I worked for, appearing corporate at all times was part of the daily grind. The solution to every marketing problem was pound the phones, drive more miles, and meet more prospects. For a while I thrived on the pressure of quarterly targets, and end of quarter panic attacks.

After four years in the role, I felt trapped. I felt trapped in my career, but also within the work I was doing. I was tired of hammering the phones. I was working with the same partners each year, who would blight me with the same gripes and complaints. My attitude also suffered. I felt hard-done-to, and moaned about the people I had to work with.

In 2012, I decided the answer was to leave and work for myself. I knew that within the marketing world I *could* do many things. I knew I could provide value to the right clients.

I thought I had escaped the 'corporate grind', when actually all I had done was build a new cage for myself. I had swapped regular reliable income, for irregular unreliable income. Worst of all, I still had no idea what I really wanted to do. Or *why*.

I had always created processes in the work I had done, but the work I really wanted to do was copywriting. Not just any copywriting either, but story-based copywriting. I had a flair for creating email sequences that deliver a powerful story. The problem was that while I was good at creating processes for my AdWords work, systematising my copywriting felt like a step too far. It felt to me like there were too many variables.

In December 2015 I attended a storytelling workshop, put on by Sean D'Souza. It became apparent that Sean had arrived at the workshop with a process, and was able to teach it.

Gradually the confusion of my mid-twenties life crisis gave way to a more singular focus. Slowly, I realised I wanted to help companies who sold transformational products and services. My work now is to help these people tell their story, and pull interested prospects into their world.

Notes

This a rebirth example of my own story, slotted into the five stage rebirth framework. To me, fitting a full rebirth plot into a single email feels a little squashed. Like most of the plot archetypes, this story could be expanded into a full email sequence.

The rebirth plot is typically one you might include in a welcome sequence after people first opt-in to your marketing. Typically this would make a good three-part series, showing your initial progress, your dark entrapment, and your final redemption.

Stages Walkthrough

Stage 1: Young hero or heroine falls under the spell of a dark power
Stage 2: Dream stage
Stage 3: Entrapment
Stage 4: The state of entrapment continues
Stage 5: Miraculous redemption by a 'light' character, and reunion

Subject: Finding your way

Hi ~Contact.FirstName~,

A lot of people talk about going through a 'mid-life crisis'. What nobody tells you when growing up is there is also another crisis in life to endure. The 'mid-twenties crisis'.

(Start of Stage 1)

In my early twenties I consumed as much marketing information as I could take on. I followed all of the 'gurus'. I studied web design, copywriting, SEO and PPC. I managed to know it all, while at the same time achieving little.

(End of Stage 1)

In stage 1 I manage to fall under the 'dark spell' of marketing. Without realising it, marketing threatens to take over my life and hijack part of my identity.

(Start of Stage 2)

In 2007 I decided to put my infinite wisdom to some use, and accepted a marketing job with a small software company. At the company I worked for, appearing corporate at all times was part of the daily grind. The solution to every marketing problem was pound the phones, drive more miles, and meet more prospects. For a while I thrived on the pressure of quarterly targets, and end of quarter panic attacks.

(End of Stage 2)

In the dream stage things start to go well, although the success I achieved came in a way that was incongruent to my real self.

(Start of Stage 3)

After four years in the role, I felt trapped. I felt trapped in my career, but also within the work I was doing. I was tired of hammering the phones. I was working with the same partners each year, who would blight me with the same gripes and complaints. My attitude also suffered. I felt hard-done-to, and moaned about the people I had to work with.

(End of Stage 3)

In stage 3, the character of the hero becomes frozen in a dark state. I didn't like the person I had become, but I didn't know how to change it.

(Start of Stage 4)

In 2012, I decided the answer was to leave and work for myself. I knew that within the marketing world I *could* do many things. I knew I could provide value to the right clients.

I thought I had escaped the 'corporate grind', when actually all I had done was build a new cage for myself. I had swapped regular reliable income, for irregular unreliable income. Worst of all, I still had no idea what I really wanted to do. Or *why*.

I had always created processes in the work I had done, but the work I really wanted to do was copywriting. Not just any copywriting either, but story-based copywriting. I had a flair for creating email sequences that deliver a powerful story. The problem was that while I was good at creating processes for my AdWords work, systematising my copywriting felt like a step too far. It felt to me like there were too many variables.

(End of Stage 4)

In stage 4 I try to escape from my dark entrapment, and if anything worsen the situation. At this point in the story it feels like one setback after another. Fundamentally, something on the inside still isn't right, which prevents any resolution.

(Start of Stage 5)

In December 2015 I attended a storytelling workshop, put on by Sean D'Souza. It became apparent that Sean had arrived at the workshop with a process, and was able to teach it.

Gradually the confusion of my mid-twenties life crisis gave way to a more singular focus. Slowly, I realised I wanted to help companies who sold transformational products and services. My work now is to help these people tell their story, and pull interested prospects into their world.

(End of Stage 5)

Finally, in stage 5 a light character comes along to liberate the hero, or in my case supply the missing piece to the puzzle.

Part 3 Summary

All seven plots look at the hero's journey from a different perspective. I don't expect all seven to be relevant to your situation, but you should have spotted one or two you can use in your marketing.

Often, these plots are more effective when they are told to completion over a longer format. For example, you might split an 'Overcoming the Monster' story into three emails. When you're creating an archetypal story, don't worry so much about email length. If you follow the plot outline and employ intrigue and suspense, your readers will keep reading to the end. Plus you can also split the story into multiple instalments.

At this point, what I would really love is for you to put this book down, and put what you have learnt so far into action. Pick a plot archetype you want to write an email about. Follow the steps outlined in Part 2 of this book, then send me your story (info@truestoryselling.com). I'll provide brief feedback and pointers on things you might want to improve.

I normally charge for that service, but it's a small gift for completing this book.

Conclusions

"Nobody arrives in heaven on a feather bed" (Cardinal Wolsey in *The Tudors*).

Weaving stories into your marketing isn't easy, but it can be done. Mastering the techniques in this book will set your marketing apart. In a way, you now have a big advantage over your competitors.

Attracting and keeping the attention of potential customers has always been the biggest marketing problem, and I suspect it always will be. New tools, techniques and fads will always offer magic 'push button' solutions, but in my view nothing keeps attention as well as a story. Yes, it's hard work getting it all down on paper (or into email). But nobody else on the planet has your story. Competitors can copy your products and steal your pricing, but they can never copy your story.

Reading a story can introduce a trance-like state of attention, like a dream. Stories can do this because they are rooted in a level of unconscious thinking. Stories are food for the unconscious part of your mind; the limbic system that deals with trust, emotions, relationships.

Every good story is really about becoming conscious. About developing awareness outside of yourself. This is what the hero's journey illustrates; the journey from childhood to adulthood. From inexperience to experience. From darkness to light. From egocentricity to empathy. From limited understanding, to 'seeing whole'. Your stories are not boring. Your stories will always be interesting, especially if you can tell them within an archetypal structure.

Stories are still the best tool for building real connections (even virtual ones). I would argue that in today's constantly connected but never engaged world, there has never been a greater need for good stories.

The real skill of a storyteller is to find new outward clothing in which to dress up a theme that already runs in the mind of your reader. Your readers already have the archetypal themes running in their heads. The 'overcoming the monster' theme is already active. The 'rags to riches' theme is already active. It's far more effective to write a story that taps into these themes. In a way, you're joining a conversation that is already happening in your reader's head.

In the last 200 years, many storytellers have produced stories that run against the plot archetypes. Christopher Booker gives numerous examples in his book, but the quintessential example to me is Samuel Beckett's play *Waiting for Godot*. First performed in 1953, *Waiting for Godot* follows two characters who are waiting for a third character, Godot, to arrive. Godot never does arrive, and the play ends.

The point about the play is there is no story. Samuel Beckett somehow managed to get away with this. You cannot.

Stories can go wrong when they are hijacked by the ego of the writer. You could argue that much of the modern technology we base our lives around fosters a sense of individualism and egocentricity. The mass production of the car led to widespread adoption of private transport. It's possible to spend all day in your car, wrapped up in your own bubble. You're seeing people, as you drive past, but there's a telling plane of glass between you and them.

I've now worked for 15 hours today. In that time I have taken three phone calls and had one Skype conversation. The only person I've spoken to in person has been my wife, Linzi. Thirty years ago it would have been impossible to get through a fifteen-hour work day by only speaking in person to one breathing human.

We're better connected online than ever before. We have more

Facebook connections than ever before. And yet so many people have never felt so lonely. Because of this isolation, people *want* to hear your story when it is told effectively, and they *want* to connect with you if you can find a way to reach them.

Real human connection is the goal here. Stories are about communicating *what* you do, but more importantly about communicating *why*. Effectively communicating *why* you are in business gives you a solid basis to communicate *what* you do.

All of the plot archetypes require a degree of humility to work, or a willingness to laugh at yourself. They all expose you in some way, making you appear vulnerable. It is this vulnerability which creates real human connection. As you write, it is hard to keep your ego from sabotaging this vulnerability.

You may remember that I do archery at weekends. In archery, there is an idea called 'zen archery'. In zen archery, the archer's goal is to eliminate egotistic concerns about the outcome of the shot. In other words, to focus exclusively on shot execution, without caring where the arrow ultimately lands.

I never get very close to 'zen', because my fragile ego gets hurt every time I miss the target. Internally I sigh or tut, even when I have executed the shot well.

The challenge when you are writing is to be aware of your ego, and keep it in check. Keeping your ego in check allows you to truly think about your reader rather than yourself. You can never climb into the head of your reader when you are wrapped up in your own tribulations.

You won't use the plot archetypes described in this book all of the time. Writing an archetypal story requires more time and effort to produce than a stereotypical story about more mundane every day events. But I hope you can now see how *elements* of the plot archetypes can be woven into your writing.

There will be one or two key places in your marketing where you should build out an archetypal series of emails. Often this is a welcome sequence, just after a contact has opted into your marketing. If you want to focus your efforts, start on this first. Pick a plot you like, and get to work.

Also, don't limit your storytelling to emails. If you give presentations or write letters, try using these techniques in other formats. The principles discussed in this book are universal.

If you have found this book interesting and useful, you should consider taking my copywriting course, Nurture Email Mastery (www.truestoryselling.com/writers). Nurture Email Mastery is a five-week 'look over my shoulder' video course, with hands-on support.

Above all, I hope you have found this inspiring, and I hope you put the information in this book to profitable use.

Action Steps

- Pick the plot archetype that most resonates with your business situation

- Write out an archetypal story, following the seven production steps

- Sign-up to my daily newsletter, and see how I put these principles into action (www.truestoryselling.com/daily)

- Develop your storytelling skills further with my video course Nurture Email Mastery (www.truestoryselling.com/writers)

Get the 'Done For You' Version

If you like the idea of telling your story but don't want to do the work yourself, I have a done-for-you service called Uncover Your Story.

In Uncover Your Story, I listen to your full story for as long as it takes to tell it. I speak to your colleagues and customers, to find out which parts of your story resonate with *them*. Then I write a concise plan for how I think you should use your story in your marketing.

What you get is absolute clarity about which parts of your story to tell, in what places. Sometimes I'll suggest that you tell your story through emails. Sometimes I'll suggest that you write a book. Sometimes I'll suggest you send direct mail. It all depends on your audience. With the plan in place, you'll know when to *stop* telling your story, and how to link to your core message.

The plan you get is your intellectual property, meaning you can implement it any way you like. Some clients choose to hire me to write their story. Some clients write it themselves, under my guidance. Some clients take the plan to a more local copywriter. I've seen all of these outcomes work effectively.

More details at www.truestoryselling.com/uncover.

Appendix

My client's original email used in my tragedy example is copied below. It's worth comparing his version with mine to see how the structure of the emails differ. I've essentially used his content, but repurposed it within the archetypal plot framework.

Subject: When no rope can be best…

Hey ~Contact.FirstName~,

2002, Mount Hood, Oregon. 6 Climbers are descending after a successful summit of the mountain. The top person on the highest rope team slips and begins to slide down the mountain. By the time the rope comes tight, he is going about 30 miles an hour. His teammate, who is in self arrest position, ostensibly to stop his climbing partner's slide, is ripped from his stance. Soon, the third member of the rope team is pulled from his self arrest position, and the three are hurtling down the side of the mountain.

1997, Ptarmigan Peak, Alaska. A team of 12 students and 2 instructors are descending after a successful summit of the mountain. The top person on the highest rope team slips and begins to slide down the mountain. By the time the rope comes tight, he is going about 30 miles an hour. His teammate, who is in self arrest position, ostensibly to stop his climbing partner's slide, is ripped from his stance. Soon, the third member of the rope team is pulled from his self arrest position, and the three are hurtling down the side of the mountain.

2002, Michimauido, Peru. Two teams of climbers, each with two members are descending after a successful summit of the mountain. The top person on the highest rope team slips and begins to slide down the mountain. By the time the rope comes tight, he is going about 30 miles an hour. His teammate, who is in self arrest position, ostensibly to stop his climbing partner's slide, is ripped from his stance. Immediately both are hurtling down the side of the mountain.

RUNP. Roped up, no protection. That's what Accidents in North American Mountaineering, a book published every year that summarizes and looks at the root cause of mountaineering accidents, calls this type of fall. It's so common that there is an abbreviation. RUNP.

A group of climbers is travelling in terrain too steep to self arrest. But they stay roped up. And choose not to place any pro. Then one slips. Because they're tied together, a second is pulled off. A third.

Time is of the essence. It always is. If you belayed everything out, you'd never get anywhere. Maybe you should use running pro. Or maybe no rope at all.

2002, Mount Hood, Oregon. 9 climbers lie in a tangled heap in a crevasse. While falling, one rope team tangled up with a second, and then a third. Like a bad Wile E. Coyote cartoon, the group tangled up into a giant ball of yarn and hurtled down the mountain until they came rest in the crevasse. 2 are dead. 5 more are seriously injured. The rescue helicopter, sent up in windy conditions, crashed killing the pilot.

1997, Ptarmigan Peak, Alaska. 12 climbers lie in a tangled heap at the base of the mountain. While falling, one rope team tangled up with a second, and then a third. Like a bad Wile E. Coyote cartoon, the group tangled up into a giant ball of yarn and hurtled down the mountain until they came rest at the base of the peak. 2 are dead. 9 more are seriously injured.

At 2 AM, about 30 miles away, a helicopter lands on the Eklutna Glacier. It's there to get Deb Ajango, the director of the Outdoor Program for Alaska Pacific University. She's had the job a week.

2002, Michimauido, Peru. 4 climbers lie in a tangled heap at the base of the mountain. While falling, one rope team tangled up with the second. Like a bad Wile E. Coyote cartoon, the group tangled up into a giant ball of yarn and hurtled down the mountain until they came rest. None survive, although rescuers suspect that 2 of the climbers survived the fall, but later died of exposure.

We use climbing ropes to make us safer. This much should be obvious. Less obvious are the several ways a rope can be used to make you safer.

You can use a traditional belay, where one climber waits at the bottom and feeds out rope to the climber. If they slip, the climber at the bottom catches her fallen friend.

You can use running protection, where both climbers climb at the same time, but clip the rope to something while they go. Here, if someone falls, you might get pulled off your stance, but the protection should hold you and save you.

You can travel in "glacier travel" mode, where you walk along, tied to someone, and if you fall, they act as your anchor.

You can short rope, where a rope is used to correct a slip before it becomes a fall.

These are all used, and are quite appropriate at various times.

But sometimes the rope makes things more dangerous.

You're climbing, tied to another member of your party. It's not very steep, so you don't take the time to put in any protection. If my partner falls, you think, I can self arrest and stop their fall.

Then the climbing route gets a bit steeper, but you don't notice. Or you think that you can still self arrest. Or it's getting late.

It doesn't really matter. You don't put in any protection. You are the anchor.

And then your partner falls. He doesn't stop. You curse and get in self arrest position. But his momentum is too much, and you're pulled off. You are hurtling off the mountain.

Decisions, decisions...

If you compare the email above to my version, I've focused on the experience of the rope team. I've also limited the email to just one story, which I think is more effective than several fragmented examples.

I've included the original email here to show how you can take an existing story and retrofit it into the archetypal framework. You don't always have to start from scratch.

About The Author

I grew up in Northern England, on a small peninsula near Liverpool called The Wirral. I spent much of my time playing snooker, watching Tranmere Rovers and avoiding school rugby training.

I now live in Sheffield, where I went to university. Sheffield has great beer and good walks. Plus the world snooker championship is held here. Sadly however, you won't see me competing anytime soon.

As I write these words in early 2017, we're about to move to Florence, Italy. Just for two months, to see how things go. I speak a little bit of Spanish, and a small but growing amount of Italian.

Other than a part-time job at a garden centre I've always worked in marketing. I've done just about every digital marketing job you can imagine, with every kind of client you can possibly imagine. My first real business success was managing Google AdWords campaigns. Later on I focused on CRM, specialising in the CRM system Infusionsoft. I realised in this time was that many companies do great things, but struggle to produce good content.

My real skill is bringing complex topics to life with engaging content.

I have an interest in history, archaeology and literature. These topics often crop up in my writing. I don't believe marketing should ever be viewed in isolation. Marketing is a deep and interesting topic when you weave together insights from other fields.

Above all, I believe good marketing should communicate who you are and what you believe in, not just what you do. I believe your line of work should be something you feel deeply passionate about. Something you have deliberately decided to do, not accidentally fallen into.

Away from work I shoot my longbow, ride motorbikes, and run barefoot. I love techno music and classical music, which most people think is an odd combination. I try to walk whenever I can. To me, running and walking is an essential part of the human experience.

If I never had to work again, I would still write every day. Or at least every other day, in between snooker sessions...

You can sign up for my daily email list at www.truestoryselling.com/daily.

Printed in Great Britain
by Amazon